# SALISBURY CATHEDRAL

*The New Bell's Cathedral Guides*

| | |
|---|---|
| Canterbury Cathedral | Reverend Canon D. Ingram Hill |
| Coventry Cathedral | John Thomas |
| St Paul's Cathedral | Peter Burman |
| Wells Cathedral | L. S. Colchester |
| Westminster Abbey | Christopher Wilson |
| | Pamela Tudor-Craig |
| | Richard Gem |
| | John Physick |

*To be published in Spring 1988*

| | |
|---|---|
| Durham Cathedral | Eric Cambridge |
| Lincoln Cathedral | David Stocker |
| York Minster | John Hutchinson and David O'Connor |

*The New Bell's Cathedral Guides*

# SALISBURY CATHEDRAL

Roy Spring

UNWIN HYMAN
London   Sydney

First published in Great Britain by Unwin Hyman
an imprint of Unwin Hyman Limited 1987

UNWIN HYMAN
Denmark House, 37–39 Queen Elizabeth Street,
London SE1 2QB

and 40 Museum Street, London WC1A 1LU

ALLEN & UNWIN Australia Pty Ltd
8 Napier Street, North Sydney, NSW 2060, Australia

ALLEN & UNWIN New Zealand Ltd with the Port Nicholson Press,
60 Cambridge Terrace, Wellington, New Zealand

ISBN 0–04–440016 0 (cased)
      0–04–440013 6 (limp)

**British Library Cataloguing in Publication Data**

Spring, Roy
    Salisbury Cathedral.——(The New Bell's
    cathedral guides)
    1. Salisbury Cathedral——Guide-books
    I. Title
    914.23'19   DA690.S16

Designed by Janet Tanner
Typeset by Latimer Trend & Company Ltd, Plymouth
Printed and bound in Great Britain at
the University Press, Cambridge.

*M. J. Sparks*

# CONTENTS

*Chapter One*

# HISTORY OF THE CATHEDRAL CHURCH OF SALISBURY

(Dedicated to the Virgin Mary and founded for secular canons)

THE STORY OF the present cathedral begins at Old Sarum, an area some one and a half miles ($2\frac{1}{2}$ km) north of Salisbury. Surrounded by an Iron Age ditch, and containing the ruins of a Norman castle and the foundations of the first cathedral (laid out by the Department of the Environment), it reveals little of its former importance.

Old Sarum contained a staging post and fort during the Roman occupation, with several roads meeting in the immediate area. The early Christian development took place away from Old Sarum. Initially part of the vast diocese administered from Dorchester in Oxfordshire, it became successively part of Winchester and then Ramsbury dioceses. The new diocese of Sarum was formed some time around 1050. Certainly by the time Herman became Bishop of Sherborne in 1058 the two sees of Ramsbury and Sherborne had been joined with Sherborne at the centre of the new diocese for some time.

After the Norman Conquest there began a redevelopment of Old Sarum with the building of a castle which became the seat of the sheriff. The Council of London in 1075 decreed that the seat of bishops should no longer be in villages or small towns but in larger places of settlement. Herman, to comply with this, chose to move to Old Sarum. Plans were laid for a

*A view of Old Sarum from the air.*

new cathedral but the main building work was to take place during the period of Bishop Osmund (1078–99).

Osmund was possibly the nephew of William I. A fifteenth-century statement also ascribes him as being the son of Henry, Count of Séez in Normandy and of having become Earl of Dorset before entering the Church. The evidence for this is unreliable. Osmund was, however, Chancellor of England under William I. Responsible for the building of the cathedral at Old Sarum, he also formulated the constitution under which the cathedral was organized, and standardized the form of service which became known as the Use of Sarum and was widely adopted.

The cathedral was consecrated in 1092 and within a week a storm had wrecked the central tower.

Osmund died in 1099 and the see remained vacant for seven years since Bishop Roger was appointed in 1102 but not consecrated until 1107. Although beginning his life in the church as a poor priest, Roger rose to be wealthy and powerful. He rebuilt the eastern end of the cathedral and built cloisters and a palace. He added the castle at Old Sarum to those of Devizes and Malmesbury already in his possession. Two events created the problems that were eventually going to lead to the removal of the cathedral from Old Sarum to another site. One was the building of the cathedral within the precincts of the castle; the other was Roger's falling into disfavour and having all his possessions pass into the hands of the king. From this time the castellan or constable of the castle was a royal appointment with power over the whole of Old Sarum.

The rebuilding of the cathedral was paid for by Bishop Roger and his fall from grace resulted in the nave remaining in its original form. The foundations of the cathedral, as laid out by the Department of the Environment, can be seen and the first and second building periods are clearly marked.

An uneasy peace was maintained during the latter half of the twelfth century under Bishops Jocelin and Hubert Walter. When Pope Honorius III laid an Interdict over England during the reign of King John, life at Old Sarum became difficult for the clergy.

Bishop Herbert Poore (1194–1217) made attempts to have the cathedral removed from Old Sarum to another site but with little success. In 1215, after a Rogation-tide procession to St Martin's Church, the gates had been closed against the canons. The Bishop calmed their fears by assuring them that the cathedral would be moved from Old Sarum. When Herbert died in 1217 he had already moved to Wilton, which was one of the possible sites for a new cathedral. Herbert Poore was succeeded by his half-brother, Richard, in 1217. Two years earlier Richard had been consecrated Bishop of Chichester. It was under the guidance and motivation of Richard Poore that Old Sarum was abandoned by the clergy and a new cathedral built in the valley below.

A petition of March 1217 outlines the grievances of the canons, and they are many. The noise of the wind blowing drowned the sound of prayers and singing. The grassless area of white chalk caused blindness! The shortage of water caused great expense because it had to be fetched from the river some distance away. But the most important reason was the

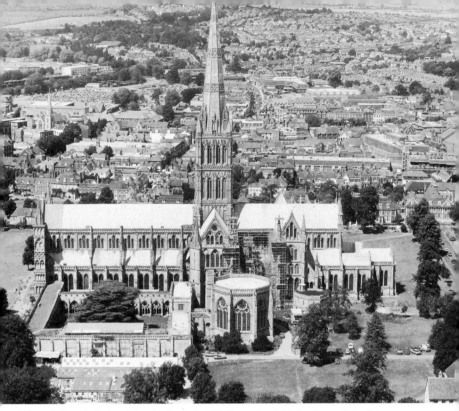

*View of the cathedral and the city beyond. Old Sarum is visible in the top left of the picture.*

restriction of movement in and out of the cathedral precincts which had to have the blessing of the castellan. It would seem that a good case was made, for in March 1218 a Papal Bull was issued giving authority to Bishop Poore to build a new cathedral away from Old Sarum.

The fact that Bishop Poore owned the site of the new cathedral, as part of his manor of Milford, is too simple a story. Legend demands a more dramatic explanation of the choosing of the site.

One story told of how Bishop Poore had a vision of the Virgin Mary in a dream and was instructed to build the new cathedral in Myr-field. Richard Poore, like his half-brother Herbert, was a frequent visitor to the Abbey of Wilton. Wilton was an important centre and the Abbey Church could have been extended to become the new cathedral. His visits to the Abbess at Wilton had not gone unnoticed and gossips were at work. The Bishop, overhearing two women discussing his visits, heard one suggest that he should build in the valley on his own ground, Myr-field. He then realized that this was the place the Virgin had suggested.

A second story tells of how a bowman stood on the ramparts of Old Sarum and fired an arrow into the air: where it landed the cathedral would be built. To account for the distance, a fourteenth-century writer explains how the arrow hit a deer which ran until dying on the site where the cathedral was built.

The valley in which the cathedral was built, and where the new city of Salisbury was laid out, is in the western part of an area bounded by the rivers Avon and Bourne. The southern boundary is where the Avon changes direction after joining with the Nadder and flows eastward to join the Bourne. Rivers on three sides ensured that shortage of water would be no problem. To the east was the Church of St Martin, with its collection of dwellings, and a marsh known as Bugmore.

In 1219 work had started, for in this year a chapel was built and a cemetery laid out. The exact site of these is not known but the fifteenth-century chantry of Bishop Beauchamp, built on the south side of the Trinity Chapel, had burials beneath its foundations. During its demolition in the eighteenth century, remains were found that must have pre-dated the chantry. This area to the south of the Trinity Chapel still remains a burial ground.

Salisbury is unique amongst English cathedrals. It was constructed in a short period of time, in one continuous operation and in a unity of style. There were no long periods when building stopped, and no drastic change in architectural design. It is this unity of design and almost perfect symmetry that gives Salisbury its distinctive quality amongst English cathedrals. After its completion no major alterations or additions took place.

Foundation stones were laid on 28 April, 1220. The ceremony is recorded in a manuscript by William de Wanda, who was precentor and then dean. Part of the description, as quoted by Francis Price, reads: 'On the day appointed for the purpose the bishop came with great devotion, few earls or barons of the country, but a great multitude of the common people coming in from all parts; and when divine service had been performed, and the Holy Spirit invoked, the said bishop, putting off his shoes, went in procession with the clergy of the church to the place of foundation singing the litany; the litany being ended and a sermon first made to the people, the bishop laid the first stone for our Lord the Pope Honorius, and the second for the

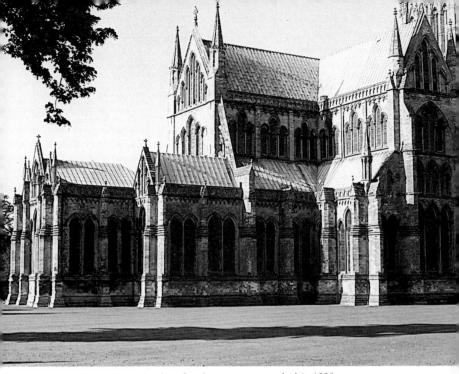

*The eastern end, where foundation stones were laid in 1220.*

Lord Stephen Langton, Archbishop of Canterbury and Cardinal of the Holy Roman Church, at that time with our Lord the King in the Marches of Wales; then he added to the new fabric a third stone for himself; William Longespée, Earl of Sarum, who was then present, laid the fourth stone and Elaide Vitri (more usually known as Ela), Countess of Sarum, the wife of the said earl, a woman truly pious and worthy because she was filled with the fear of the Lord, laid the fifth. After her, certain noblemen, each of them added a stone; then the dean, the chantor, the chancellor, the archdeacons and canons of the church of Sarum who were present did the same, amidst the acclamations of multitudes of the people weeping for joy and contributing thereto their alms with a ready mind according to the ability which God had given them. But in the process of time the nobility being returned from Wales, several of them came thither, and laid a stone, binding themselves to some special contribution for the whole seven years following.'

To finance the building work Bishop Poore apportioned part of his income to the fabric fund. He also ensured that all the canons did likewise. At a chapter meeting on 15 August, 1220, the rules were laid down relating to the canons' contributions. These provide for action being taken should money not be forthcoming. Any canon who neglected to pay his due fifteen days after the time stipulated in his agreement was liable to have the corn on his prebend seized and sold to raise the stipulated sum. Failing these measures, the Bishop held the threat of excommunication. By these means and by good administration, the work proceeded well. By 1225 the first section of the eastern end was complete, namely the eastern chapel, the ends of the choir aisles and at least part of the eastern bay of the presbytery. On the eve of Michaelmas-day (30 September) 1225, Bishop Poore consecrated three altars, one to the Holy Trinity and All Saints, one to St Stephen and one to St Peter. Present at the ceremony were the Bishop of Dublin and Stephen Langton, Archbishop of Canterbury. Daily worship was now possible in at least part of the new cathedral, continuing to the present day. William Longespée, Earl of Salisbury, and half-brother to King John, died in March 1226 and was the first person to be buried in the newly completed Trinity Chapel. On 18 July, 1226, the bodies of three Old Sarum bishops were translated to the new cathedral.

The building of the cathedral continued under the guidance of Nicholas of Ely and Elias of Dereham until 1246. This combination of master mason and clerk of the works saw the completion of much of the main part of the cathedral, certainly to the commencement of the base of the west front.

Of the people connected with the early building work Elias of Dereham is the most interesting. Coming from West Dereham, he had been a friend of Hubert Walter, who became Archbishop of Canterbury. It was Hubert who brought Elias to Old Sarum in 1189 when Hubert became Bishop of Salisbury. Elias eventually became a canon of the cathedral, holding the prebend of Beaminster Secunda. He was also a canon of Wells Cathedral and was known to Adam Locke, master mason at Wells.

Elias spent some time in France with Stephen Langton during the Archbishop's voluntary exile. Langton at one time referred to Elias as the only honest man in England. This statement is supported by some of the tasks entrusted to Elias. He administered the wills of three archbishops and took over administration of the church during the interregnum periods. At Runnymede in 1215 he was given charge of some four copies of Magna Carta to deliver to various places; at Oxford he was given six more and, therefore, delivered the bulk of the

Charter copies. This then was the man who became the first clerk of the works.

Richard Poore was translated to Durham in 1228, leaving Bishop Robert Bingham to continue the work. Poore's connection with Durham is associated with the rebuilding of the eastern end of the cathedral. Much has been said in the past suggesting that Bishop Poore may have taken Elias of Dereham with him to Durham, also that Elias designed the Chapel of the Nine Altars. Elias may have visited Durham but there is no evidence of his connection with the new east end. The work was not started until after Poore's death.

Bishop Bingham had been a canon at Old Sarum and had, therefore, seen the move and the beginnings of the building work. He died in 1246, the same year as the master mason and the clerk of the works. Apart from his interest in the building of the cathedral, Bingham is probably best known for having the Harnham bridge built, thus providing Salisbury with a direct route to the south. The effect of the bridge was felt by the people of Wilton since it drew away their trade.

Despite the deaths of three of the most important people in the same year, the construction of the cathedral continued. Robert the mason took charge of the work and combined the posts of master mason and clerk of the works. Nothing is known of the background of Robert or how long he was in charge of the work. It must be assumed that he saw the completion of the nave.

William of York became Bishop in 1247. Although Godwin described him as 'a courtier from his childhood, and better versed in the laws of the realm, which he had chiefly studied, than in the laws of God', he supported the building work but died in 1256 two years before the first consecration of the cathedral. In 1248 Bishop William of York allowed the Dean and Chapter to have a strip of land wide enough for the building of the south walk of the cloisters which by then were under construction. By 1248 the wall of the west front was already built above the level of the cloister. Two windows in the south west staircase are covered by the west wall of the cloister. This was due to the enlargement of the cloister area from the original plan.

By 1256 the main walls were complete and the covering of the roofs with lead took place at the start of the episcopate of Giles de Bridport. He had held a prebend at Wells and became dean in 1253. During part of this period Roger, a canon of

13

Salisbury for eighteen years, became Bishop of Wells. This connection between Salisbury and Wells was only one of several during the building of the cathedral.

Recorded at Wells Cathedral is the loan of certain books to the Dean and Chapter of Salisbury Cathedral. These books had been used in part to determine the layout of the sculptures on Wells' west front and it is presumed that Salisbury wanted them for the same purpose. It is difficult to know what influence they had on the west front but they may have influenced the Old Testament frieze in the Chapter House. It took Wells ninety years to get back the books.

By 1258 the cathedral was complete insofar as the main walls and roofs were finished. Bishop Bridport organized the 'hallowing' of the new building by Boniface, Archbishop of Canterbury, on the 20 September, 1258. The cathedral was not complete for a note from the appendix to statutes of Bishop Mortival states that 'the Church of Sarum was commenced building in the time of King Richard, and continued through the reign of three kings, and was completed on the 25th March in the year 1266, the whole expense of the fabric up to that time having been forty-two thousand marks'.

Forty-six years of continuous building work represents a great deal of effort on the part of the builders. It had meant the extraction of some 60,000 tons (60,960 tonnes) of stone from the mines at Chilmark and its transportation the 12 miles (19 km) to Salisbury. Between March and October each year there would have to be ten cartloads each day arriving on site. One of those present at the laying of the foundations who pledged to help the work was Alice Brewer or Briwere. She owned the manor of Worth Matravers in south Dorset and stone quarries at Downshay. It was from these quarries that she pledged a gift of Purbeck marble for the first twelve years of the building work. For this reason the cathedral contains large quantities of this shelly limestone, which by virtue of its taking a high polish has been termed marble. The quarries, or more correctly, the mines, at Downshay produced some 12,000 tons (12,192 tonnes) of stone for Salisbury, all of which found its way from Poole Harbour to Christchurch and then up the Avon to Salisbury. The roofs of the cathedral contain approximately 2,800 tons (2,840 tonnes) of timber. Four hundred tons (406 tonnes) of lead were used to cover the roofs and glaziers filled three-quarters of an acre ($\frac{1}{3}$ hectare) of windows with glass.

These are only some of the materials used during the first fifty years of the building work. Even quantities such as these mean little until one realizes the physical effort required to convert the stone, wood, lead and glass into a fit state to be included in the building. To ensure the supply of materials, the efficient spending of money, to arrange the employment of suitable craftsmen and to control the quality of the work called for someone with authority, a knowledge of all the crafts and the motivation to produce a work of art and a house of prayer.

The date from the Statutes of Bishop Mortival of 1266 may suggest that the whole of the cathedral, including cloisters and Chapter House, was finished by that time. A date of 1280 for the Chapter House has been used, based on coins of this date having been found in the foundations during later work. Without doubt, the whole of the cathedral buildings, with the exception of the tower and spire, were finished by 1280, including the treasury and the muniment room, added late in the thirteenth century against the south wall of the south-east transept.

During this main period of building work a detached bell tower was constructed to the north of the cathedral. There are no precise dates for the period of its construction but from illustrations and known details, there is little doubt of its having been built between 1230 and 1260.

There has been a great deal of conjecture about the building of the tower and spire, both the date and the man responsible. The more popular choice of date is 1330–60. The choice of this period is based on a document binding Richard of Farley to carry out certain works. The agreement is a standard one, giving details of how the job is to be controlled and the salary to be paid. Richard of Farley was connected with work in Bath and at Reading at about the same time, so would, presumably, not have been able to give continuous supervision.

In 1329 the Dean and Chapter obtained permission to build a wall around the Close. A licence was granted to the Chapter in 1331 for the cathedral at Old Sarum to be demolished and the materials used for building work at the new cathedral. This combination of permission for enclosure, the provision of building materials from Old Sarum and the engagement of Richard of Farley all seem to come together for one purpose: and that was not the building of the tower and spire but the Close wall.

Contained in the Close wall are numerous fragments of Old

*The cathedral from the south-west.*

Sarum Cathedral; within the tower and spire none has been found. From 1330 the Dean and Chapter's records are complete but no mention is made of the building of a tower and spire. Deans and bishops up to 1310 are remembered in the list of benefactors of the fabric, none during the rest of the fourteenth century. The designer of the tower and spire may well remain unknown for any name put forward can only be speculative.

As the construction of the tower progressed, buttresses were built within the triforium and clerestory against the springing points of the main crossing arches. By 1320 the eastern crossing had been reinforced with bracing to prevent eastward movement of the choir. External buttressing of the nave came at a later date.

Two bishops dominated the fourteenth and fifteenth centuries. Robert Wyville, 1330–75, the longest serving bishop, occupied the period during which, according to some, the spire was built. Walsingham writes of him as 'illiterate and so little favoured by nature that had the pope seen him, he would never have been raised to so high a dignity'. He did, however, succeed in getting Sherborne Castle back into the keeping of the bishops of Salisbury. The castle had been taken into royal keeping at the time of Bishop Roger's fall from grace. Wyville spent time and money fortifying his manors of Salisbury, Woodford, Sherborne, Chardstock, Potterne, Canning, Sunning and his mansion in Fleet Street. His grave slab and brass are in the north-east transept.

Problems arose from the building of the tower and spire for, in 1387, it was recorded at a Chapter Meeting that the spire threatened to ruin the cathedral. The Bishop, Ralph Erghum, granted indulgences to all those who helped with its repair. At this same meeting the canonization of Osmund was discussed and marks the beginning of the final stages in gaining recognition for Osmund.

In 1394 Nicholas Portland was engaged as master mason and it has been suggested that this marked the beginning of the building of the bracing arches at the central crossing. Robert Wayte, who became master mason in 1415, might also have been responsible for the crossing arches.

In 1423 it is recorded that 'the stone tower in the middle of Salisbury Cathedral is ruinous' and an annual grant of £50 was made to repair it. Again, in 1429, certain tithes were used for the maintenance of the spire.

An iron chantry chapel was built in the second bay of the nave from the east on the north side. The ironwork was made by John Ewley of Bristol in 1430 and enclosed the burial place of Walter Lord Hungerford and his wife.

In 1450 Richard Beauchamp was translated from Hereford to Salisbury, where he remained bishop for thirty-two years. It was during this period that success was finally achieved in obtaining the canonization of Osmund, for which various efforts had been made since 1228 although Osmund had been regarded as a saint since his death in 1099. The canonization took place in 1457 and Pope Calixtus III issued a mandate to Bishop Beauchamp to prepare a shrine and translate the relics.

Beauchamp's accession to the see of Salisbury came at a troubled period. His predecessor, William Aiscough, had been murdered at Edington Priory, in the wake of the Jack Cade rebellion, and the palace at Salisbury plundered. Beauchamp proved to be a stabilizing influence and by various works left his mark on the cathedral and palace. The great hall and tower were added to the palace and in the cathedral the central crossing was put into its present form. Bracing arches were built at the north and south ends of the main transepts and vaulting was constructed at the base of the tower. The arches were added to prevent any further bending of the main piers. The vaulting (1479) replaced a wooden ceiling that had been put in position towards the end of the thirteenth century to seal off from the cathedral the building work of the tower and spire.

In 1473 Beauchamp was appointed master and surveyor of the king's works at Windsor, which involved the rebuilding of St George's Chapel. Before his death in 1481, he had built a chantry at Salisbury. It was to the south of the Trinity Chapel and had an entrace into the cathedral through the south wall of the chapel. This chantry was demolished in 1789.

Another chantry was built between 1464 and 1471 on the north side of the Trinity Chapel in which were buried Robert Lord Hungerford and his wife.

Chapter records contain an entry in 1444–5 to the effect that a library and schoolroom be built over the east walk of the cloister. The work carried over into Richard Beauchamp's time at the cathedral. The library occupied the whole of the upper part of the east cloister walk; half the building was removed in 1757.

Bishop Edmund Audley, 1502–24, built for himself, and in

honour of the Assumption of the Blessed Virgin, a chantry chapel on the north side of the presbytery.

During the Reformation Salisbury suffered certain visitations resulting in some damage being done and the removal of the cathedral's treasure. Osmund's shrine was the main victim, being destroyed and its treasure removed.

Maintenance of the fabric still proved a problem. In 1564 the canons and prebendaries agreed to pay one-tenth of their income for repair works. Each prebendary, on installation, had to pay £5 to the fabric fund.

The period of the Commonwealth was to some extent less damaging at Salisbury than in many other places. The Bishop's palace was sold off and became an inn. The Chapter House became a meeting place for the Parliamentary commissioners and suffered from iconoclastic attention, the images of God in the stone frieze being cut out.

Throughout the period, workmen are said to have made repairs and looked after the fabric. In Dr Pope's 'Life of Bishop Ward', he says that when these workmen were asked by whom they were sent, they replied 'Those who employ us will pay us; trouble not yourselves to enquire; whoever they are they do not desire to have their names known.'

After the Restoration, Seth Ward was appointed Bishop and at a meeting called in May 1668 a resolution was passed that 'to prevent the ruin of the church, especially the steeple, the fifth part of the revenue of each prebendary and dignitary should be assigned for repairs. Bishop Ward, being a friend of Christopher Wren, invited him to Salisbury to inspect the cathedral. Between 1669 and 1689 Wren carried out his surveys and produced his report. The original report, sent to Bishop Ward, no longer exists and its fate could be as recorded by Aubrey. Having mentioned Wren's report, Aubrey writes: 'I asked the Bishop for it, and he told me he had lent it, to whom he could not tell, and had no copy of it.' What does exist is the notebook which contains the substance of the report, together with sketches illustrating various points.

The report is a model for others to follow because it uses simple terms to explain the problems and the proposed solutions. It begins thus: 'The whole pile is large and magnificent and may be justly accounted one of the best patterns of architecture in that age wherein it was built.' There follows a description of the cathedral, an outline of the problems and various suggestions as to repairs that should be carried out.

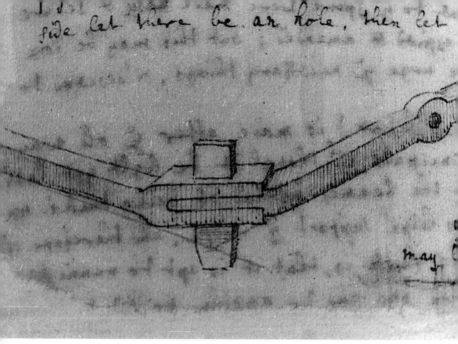

*A sketch from Christopher Wren's notebook where he describes the method by which metal bands should be joined.*

As a result of Wren's work, the first comprehensive survey of the cathedral, repairs were initiated and over a period of some sixty years gradually completed. Three cathedral clerks of the works—Thomas Naish, 1679–1714, Thomas Naish, 1736–44 and Francis Price, 1744–53—supervised many of the repairs to the cathedral, including the installation of iron reinforcing inside the tower and on the exterior of the spire. The first Thomas Naish carried out the recommended repairs to the spire, including the use of oyster shells for filling large open joints. Many shells have been found in subsequent repairs. The second Thomas Naish was responsible for the first accurate measurement of the declination of the spire. The result of these measurements can still be seen marked on the floor of the central crossing. Francis Price proved to be a surveyor of some quality and continued the repair work, in particular to the roofs. He is best remembered for his book, the first to give details of the structure.

In his book Price records an incident that could have been a major disaster. on 21 June, 1742, at about ten o'clock at night a flash of lightning was seen to strike the tower. The next morning the head verger raised the alarm as a fire had started in the bell chamber and, with a great deal of effort, the fire was put out. Repairs were carried out but Thomas Naish left one charred piece of timber as a reminder which can still be seen.

Half the library building over the east walk of the cloister was removed in 1757, the floor and roof timbers of the demolished section being used to construct the new roof. At the same time the cloister roofs were stripped of their lead and slates were fixed instead. Between 1777 and 1779 the choir was refurbished under the direction of Edward Lush, the clerk of the works.

Jacob, second Earl of Radnor, had the fifteenth-century iron chantry of Walter Lord Hungerford removed from the north side of the nave to its present position on the south side of the choir. The greatest changes to the interior and exterior of the cathedral took place between 1789 and 1793 when James Wyatt undertook to carry out improvements.

The latter half of the eighteenth century, although following a busy period earlier in the century when much work was carried out, must have been a period of neglect. The Hon. John Byng, later fifth Viscount Torrington, records a visit to Salisbury on 7 September, 1782. After settling in at the White Hart, he says: 'and then went to survey the Cathedral which I had seen before and of which I resumed my old remarks. The close is comfortable, and the divines well seated; but the house of God is kept in sad order, to the disgrace of our Church, and of Christianity. Whenever I see these things I wish for a return to the authority and Church government of a land. The church-yard is like a cow-common, as dirty and as neglected, and through the centre stagnates a boggy ditch. I wonder that the residents do not subscribe to plant near, and rowel the walks, and cleanse the ditch, which might be made an handsome canal.

'I hope that when the new Bishop arrives, who is a scholar, and a gentleman, he will be shocked at the delapidations of the beautiful old chapter house; and the cloisters; through the rubbish of which they are now making a passage for his new Lordship's installation in the Chapter House.'

This description shows clearly that all was not well. The new bishop, mentioned as being a scholar and a gentleman, was Shute Barrington, firstly Bishop of Llandaff and then moving to Salisbury in 1782.

James Wyatt carried out a survey of the cathedral and at a chapter meeting on the 26 August, 1789 it is recorded that: 'the Lord Bishop of Sarum, having caused the contracts and plans

*View of the Hungerford chapel, which formerly adjoined the north side of Salisbury cathedral.*

for the Altar Piece and Improvements of the Cathedral Church to be laid before the Chapter, and the same having been inspected and considered, after due Deliberation—Resolved, that this Chapter do approve of and authorise his Lordship to carry the same into execution.' There follows a list of work to be done, none of which appears to be too outrageous; but what followed was the gutting of a medieval building.

The thirteenth-century choir screen was removed, and the chantries of Robert Hungerford and Richard Beauchamp were demolished. From the salvaged material a new choir screen was built. During the demolition of Beauchamp's chantry, his tomb was lost and the clerk of the works, William Matthew, was dismissed. What remained of the ancient glass was removed and disposed of. All the tombs situated east of the high altar, except the Gorges and Hertford, were removed and placed in the nave arcading. The whole of the eastern vaulting was painted with lime wash, obliterating the thirteenth-century paintings. The remains of the bell tower were demolished and the churchyard cleared of headstones and grave markers. None of this work is mentioned in the account of the

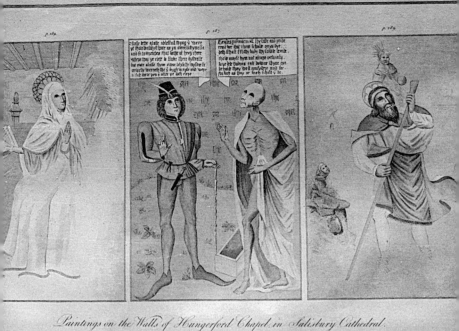

*Paintings on the walls of the Hungerford Chapel.*

chapter meeting of 26 August 1789. It is easy to understand why alterations take place as tastes change or a piece of furniture needs replacing or a new piece is required. But the wholesale removal of original fittings is difficult to understand. Some work was carried out to the spire and tower where the use of 'Roman cement' and iron cramps marks the areas repaired.

The final result of Wyatt's work was to leave the eastern end of the cathedral open from the choir screen to the east wall of the Trinity Chapel, all except five windows filled with plain glass, all the vaults lime washed, and the choir walled off at its western end with an ad hoc screen on top of which was an organ donated by George III. This is now in St Thomas' Church. There was much criticism of the work from many people, including Richard Gough of the Society of Antiquaries, who resigned from that body when Wyatt at last became a member.

Covering the vaulting of the nave and the main transepts with lime wash continued in the early years of the nineteenth century. By 1815 opinions changed and some of the old glass

23

OPPOSITE: *A photograph of c. 1860 showing the view towards the south transept. Wyatt's choir screen can be seen coming out beyond the line of the bracing arches.*

ABOVE: *A drawing of 1818 which shows how Wyatt left the whole of the eastern end of the cathedral as one open space.*

was reinstated in the west window of the nave, marking the end of a traumatic period in the cathedral's history.

Bishop Denison initiated the repair of the cloisters in 1850, when many of the original Purbeck shafts were replaced with Chilmark. Much of the cloister arcading was repaired with mortar reinforced by iron nails set into wooden plugs. The result has been the rusting of the nails, causing many areas of the masonry to split. Denison died in 1854 and is buried between his two wives under the cedar trees in the cloister garth. As a memorial to him, the Chapter House was restored under the direction of Henry Clutton between 1855 and 1856. New glazing and floor tiles were put in, the frieze of the Old Testament was restored and painted, the vault was painted and the central shaft of Purbeck marble was rebuilt. Around the top of this shaft was an iron collar, put in when the Chapter House was built and from the collar eight iron bars were taken to the angles of the building and built into the walls. Wren had remarked that this ironwork should be taken through the wall and secured by plates on the outside. This work was done early in the eighteenth century. Clutton had the ironwork removed and replaced by a band of iron immediately under the parapet on the exterior. The buttresses of the Chapter House were enlarged at the same time.

Gilbert Scott was asked to survey the cathedral and produce a report on its state. Between 1860 and 1875 the whole of the cathedral was subject to an extensive restoration. The work covered repairs to the fabric and the reinstatement of the interior.

Wyatt's screen was removed and replaced with an open-work iron screen made by Francis Skidmore. The floors of the choir and presbytery were relaid with Minton encaustic tiles. The high altar was established in the presbytery once again and backed by a reredos. An attempt was made to uncover the original paintings in the high eastern vault under Wyatt's lime wash but the pigment of the thirteenth-century paint was found to be in a friable condition. Tracings were made of the images that could be seen through the lime wash and these were developed into the present paintings, executed by Clayton and Bell.

Many of the interior Purbeck shafts and bases were repaired

*A drawing of the nave showing Wyatt's screen and the organ paid for by George III.*

and all were treated with either linseed oil or French polish, giving what has come to be known as the 'stove-pipe' effect. The exterior masonry received attention but, unfortunately, Ashburton marble was used for shafts and sills instead of Purbeck.

Two important areas received particular attention: the tower and the west front. Problems had arisen about the stability of the original lantern stage of the tower. Scott expressed concern about the safety of the lantern and, for a second opinion, the Dean and Chapter consulted Shields, who agreed with Scott's concern. A system of iron bracing was introduced into the lantern, where diagonally placed bars split into Y ends were passed round the corner stairways and connected with exterior frames. Shields' ironwork has done much to ensure the stability of this first stage of the tower. He also wanted to install a system of frame bracing into the arcading of the lantern. Unfortunately, money ran out and his idea was abandoned. The masonry of the tower was repaired and extra mullions were built on the inside of the windows in the upper stage of the tower. Although Scott spent some time looking at stone in Chilmark and Tisbury, he decided to use the bed at Chilmark that the original miners left as the roof of their mines. It has been proved that the original builders knew better than Scott about the lasting qualities of certain of the Chilmark stone. At Salisbury, as at Westminster Abbey, the stone used by Scott has decayed rapidly.

By the nineteenth century, the west front was devoid of most of the sculpture that originally filled the niches. Various prints show varying numbers of statues. Hollar in the seventeenth century shows a great many; only ten are shown on a print of 1814. Scott engaged J. F. Redfern to design and produce new statues. Redfern produced models and the majority of the carving was carried out by a local mason.

G. E. Street followed Scott as the Dean and Chapter's adviser. He carried out the restoration of the north porch in 1880, which includes a fine set of ironwork.

Structural problems still remained. Between 1903 and 1914 Wren's exterior reinforcing of the spire was replaced with horizontal exterior copper bands and the lightning conductor system was installed. Movement in the west front resulted in underpinning work being done under the direction of C. E. Ponting. Further works to the spire were carried out between 1920 and 1939.

Forsyth directed the infilling of stairways in the lantern stage of the tower and the repair of the timber frame within the spire. Between 1949 and 1951 the top 23 feet (7 metres) of the spire was rebuilt, removing an ironwork frame, together with the original iron cross. The cross had been covered with copper sheathing and a new copper vane was fitted in 1762.

During the late 1950s and early 1960s much of Scott's interior work was undone. Skidmore's screen was sold for scrap along with the Communion rails. The Minton tiles were removed and buried in the grounds of the palace. The reredos was broken up and dispersed. In the Chapter House two windows were removed and the 1860 glass destroyed. As a result of this 'Wyattism', complaints and criticism mounted, resulting in the formation of the Cathedrals' Advisory Commission, now the watchdog of what Deans and Chapters are doing. In 1980 a new east window in the Trinity Chapel was installed and the Chapter House glazing restored.

The problems still arise, major work is planned for the tower and spire, including metal bracing within the spire. The original builders were bold in their concept and daring in their execution, leaving problems for those who have followed.

## Chapter Two

# THE EXTERIOR OF THE CATHEDRAL

'THE WHOLE PILE is large and magnificent and may be justly accounted one of the best patterns of architecture in that age wherein it was built.' This extract from Christopher Wren's report sums up the first view of the cathedral from within the Close. Some five acres (two hectares) of lawn surround the cathedral, giving the impression that the 'whole pile' has been placed upon green baize.

From the north-east corner of the churchyard one can see the east end, where foundation stones were laid in 1220, and the top of the spire, finished some one hundred years later. The building rises from the east end to choir and presbytery and to tower and spire in logical sequence. Remove the tower and spire and the rest of the cathedral becomes somewhat ordinary, but with the tower and spire the rest of the architecture is held together, forming an integral part of what may, or may not, have been one grand design.

The surroundings of the cathedral add to its beauty of form, which can be viewed in comfort on three sides without the hindrance of encroaching buildings. This says much for those who planned the layout and ensured space was left to enhance the cathedral. The grassed area to the north and west of the cathedral was until the late eighteenth century a churchyard, when on Wyatt's suggestion the area was levelled, creating the lawns.

*The cathedral looking north-east.*

## The West Front

The west front contains the only exterior sculptures on the cathedral. It is a screen wall, being wider than the combined widths of nave and aisles, and was intended to take an important part in the liturgical life of the cathedral. The positioning of the nave against the west front can be seen from the positions of the buttresses. The central buttresses mark the nave arcading and the small ones the aisle walls.

The original scheme can only be surmised since no record exists of what was placed in the niches. Eight statues, or parts of statues are still in their original positions. They help to give an idea of at least part of what was intended. The Reverend H. T. Armfield, one of Scott's advisers on the replacement of statues, in his *Guide to the Statues on the west front* published in 1869, suggests that the grouping of the sculptures was based on the 'Te Deum Laudamus':

> 'To thee all angels cry aloud
>     the heavens and all the powers therein
> To thee Cherubim and Seraphim:
>     continually do cry,
> Holy, Holy, Holy:
>     Lord God of Sabaoth:
> Heaven and earth are full: of the majesty of thy glory.
> The glorious company of the apostles praise thee:
>     the goodly fellowship of the prophets praise thee;
> The noble army of martyrs praise thee;
>     the holy Church throughout all the world doth
>     acknowledge thee.'

This suggests the content of each of the tiers of statues. Starting at the top and considering the main niches only, these are a tier of angels, a tier of Old Testament patriarchs and prophets, a tier of apostles, a tier of doctors, virgins and martyrs. Finally, the bottom tier comprises eminently worthy persons connected with the Church and with the cathedral.

The front is divided vertically into seven parts: the faces of the north and south towers, the main buttresses and the areas between. There are five horizontal layers of niches for sculpture with niches on the north and south return faces and also on the eastern returns. All the niches have plinths which indicates that there may have been figures in those niches that are now empty.

*The west front.*

At the base of the west front there is the moulded plinth common to the whole cathedral. There are three entrances, each with triple gables with finials. The gables are 'roofed' with weathered stone and at the bottom of each gable slope is set a grotesque head as a water spout. The central doorway has a covered porch, part of which is formed by the roofed gables. Each gable has a niche with a carved figure and together the three figures represent the Annunciation. In the centre the Virgin carries a lily, St Gabriel is depicted in the left hand niche and St Mary in the right hand. Within the porch the arcading has marble shafting and foliated capitals. Over the west doors the outer order of moulding is delicate undercut work of foliage, flowers, animals and humans. Although restored in the nineteenth century there are original sections on which colour can still be seen. Such undercut work demands great skill and patience. This porch was known as the Blue Porch, presumably from the colour it was originally painted.

The main doors are flanked by splayed jambs with marble shafts and divided with a central cluster of shafts. Above the doors, within moulded niches, are sculptures representing the Virgin Mary holding the infant Christ flanked by censing angels. The north and south doorways have moulded quatrefoil panels in their central gables but no carvings. The north doorway was one of the more used entrances, for within the porch is a holy water stoup and at the base of the adjacent stairway a fireplace which suggests the presence of a door-keeper.

The lowest tier of figures, starting on the north tower and continuing to the south tower, are:

St Birinus *(d. 650), first bishop in Wessex.* St Etheldreda *(d. 679), foundress of the Abbey at Ely, model of church is carried.* King Henry VI *(d. 1471), founder of Eton College and Kings College, Cambridge.* Bishop Bridport *(d. 1262), present at first consecration of cathedral in 1258.* Bishop Richard Poore *(d. 1287), founder of the cathedral, a model of which is carried.* King Henry III *(d. 1272), present at dedication of Trinity Chapel, 1225.* St Edmund of Canterbury *(d. 1240), Canon and Treasurer of the cathedral 1222–34, Archbishop of Canterbury.* Bishop Odo *(d. 959), Bishop of Ramsbury 926–42.* Bishop Thomas Ken *(d. 1711), Bishop of Bath and Wells. This statue was carved by Alan Wyon in 1937.* St Osmund *(d. 1099), Bishop at Old Sarum 1078–99.* Bishop

*A water spout on the west front.*

Brithwold *(d. 1045), Bishop of Ramsbury 1005–45.* St Alban *(d. 303), first English martyr.* St Alphege *(d. 1012), Archbishop of Canterbury. The bones held in his robe indicate the manner of his martyrdom—being clubbed to death with the bones of an oxen.* St Edmund, *king and martyr (d. 870). King of East Angles 855–870.* St Thomas of Canterbury *(1170), Archbishop of Canterbury 1162–70.*

The aisle windows are of two lights with tracery. The hood mould continues but dies into the adjoining faces, leaving strange, part arcading. The windows are not central between buttresses and towers, possibly for effect when viewed from the centre of the west front.

The second tier of figures from the north face of the north tower are:

St Patrick *(fifth-century), Patron saint of Ireland.* St Ambrose *(d. 397), Bishop of Milan and one of the four 'Fathers of the Church)'.* St Jerome *(d. 420), one of the greatest scholars of his age.* St Gregory the Great *(d. 604). When Bishop of Rome, he sent Augustine to Britain as a missionary.* St Augustine of Hippo *(d. 430). Son of St Monica and author of many books.*

In 1963 the figure of St Augustine of Canterbury was removed from the front of the buttress. It was a potential danger to passers-by and disintegrated on removal.

St Remigius of Rheims *(d. 533). Apostle of the French. The Salisbury City Charter of 1229 grants a fair on his feast day, 1 October.* The Blessed Virgin Mary. *This figure has a thirteenth-century body with nineteenth-century dove, arm and head. The body is only 6 inches (15 cm) thick, making it more like a relief carving.*

Over the central doors are eleven figures, all nineteenth-century. In the wall behind these figures are moulded quatrefoils that open into the gallery below the west window. Their purpose was to allow a choir in the gallery to be heard outside. The same arrangement of gallery and openings is to be seen at Wells. The openings are now infilled with stone. At one time they were glazed but originally would have been open, the sound of voices appearing to come from the figures placed in front of the openings.

From the north the figures are:

St Barbara, *with emblems of book, and tower in which her father kept her from the sight of other men.* St Katherine of Alexandria

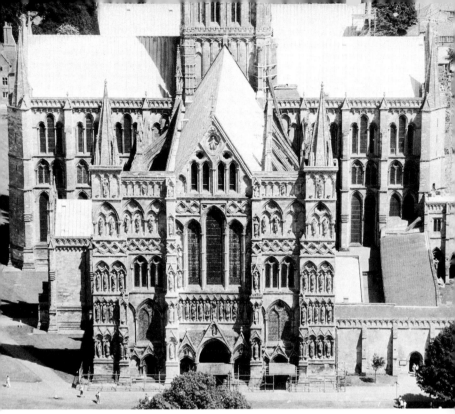

*The west front and the nave at the east end of which the original lantern can be seen.*

*(d. 310). Her emblems of wheel and sword can be seen.* St Roche *(d. 1337), patron saint of the sick.* St Nicholas of Myra *(d. 326). On his feast day the 'Boy Bishop' was elected (see p. 116).* St George of Cappadocia *(d. 303). Patron saint of England.* St Christopher *(d. 250), shown with the Christ Child on his shoulder.* St Sebastian *(d. 288), pierced with arrows.* St Cosmas *(d. 301). Patron saint of medicine.* St Damian *(d. 301). Brother of Cosmas.* St Margaret of Antioch *(d. 306). Her emblems of dagger and cross are shown.* St Ursula *(d. 451), with emblematic arrow.*

Continuing along this tier the figures are:

St John the Baptist, *thirteenth-century figure repaired in the nineteenth century.* St Stephen. *Carries stones in right hand.* St Lucy *(d. 303), emblems of lamp and dagger.* St Agatha *(d. 251), with pincers.* St Agnes *(d. 304), with her emblematic lamb.* St Cecilia *(d. 210), patroness of music and musicians. Holds model of an organ.*

37

The third tier of figures are Apostles and Evangelists. From north to south they are:

St Jude, *with halberd.* St Simon, *with saw.* St Andrew, *with cross.* St Thomas, *with a carpenter's square.* St Peter, *with keys. This is a thirteenth-century figure with nineteenth-century repairs.* St Paul, *with sword. Another figure of the thirteenth century with nineteenth-century repairs.* St James the Less, *with fuller's club.* St James the Greater, *with pilgrim's staff.* St Bartholomew, *with knife.* St Matthias, *with lance.*

The windows at this level light the ends of the nave triforium roofs. Here also is a walkway that allows access across under the west window and into the north and south stairways.

Next comes a band of moulded decoration in lozenge pattern which has cusping forming quatrefoil panels. The moulding is repeated over the top of the west window. This form of decoration is adapted on the tower and spire. On the tower the central band, between the two storeys and the parapets, shows the lozenge pattern with cusping. On the spire the three bands of decoration are another variation of the same theme.

The fourth tier of figures are prophets and patriarchs of the Old Testament. From north to south, they are:

King David, *with harp.* Moses, *with stone tablets.* Isaiah, *the prophet.* Jeremiah, *the prophet.* Ezekiel, *the prophet.* Abraham, *with knife.* Noah, *with model of ark.* Job, *the patriarch.* Daniel, *the prophet.* Samuel, *judge and prophet.* King Solomon, *with sceptre and model of the Temple.*

The fifth tier of figures comprises angels and archangels. On the face of the towers are nineteenth-century archangels, on the face of the main buttresses are two thirteenth-century angels. There are two further angels holding musical instruments, one of which is partly thirteenth-century.

In the gable are two double lancet windows that light the nave roof. A figure of Christ within a vesica is surmounted by a carving of a pelican.

All the niches on the west front and its return faces were intended to receive statues. All those niches to which access has been gained in recent years have dowel holes cut in the plinths and many have fixing holes for securing sculpture to the back wall of the niche. Scott's nineteenth-century work allowed for

*The cathedral from the east. Consecration crosses can be seen on the eastern wall where the foundations were laid in 1220.*

filling as many of the front niches as possible, but support for the scheme fell short of that expected. Statues were offered for sponsorship, angels £45, prophets etc. £55 and archangels £65. A drawing in Armfield's description of the west front has all the niches numbered, making it easy for donors to pick those sculptures for which they wanted to pay.

Gleeson White in the previous Bell's Guide spends some time in listing the criticisms of the west front. Much of this stemmed from the seeming lack of understanding about the use of the west front as a display area and the part it played in the liturgical life of the cathedral. The west front does not match the building behind it and does give a false impression of the width of the building. The entrances are insignificant compared with French cathedrals but Salisbury's main entrance was the north porch, not the centre of the west front. This central doorway was only occasionally in use for ceremonial purposes. The low feature of the entrances is in some ways a result of the gallery built in the level below the west window, the gables of the central entrance being kept below gallery level. The north and south ends, although referred to as towers, are in reality enlarged stairways topped with a spire and four spirelets. The stairways give access to gallery, triforium, clerestory and main roof. On the east return walls are three-light windows that match those of the nave clerestory and light passageways within the wall thickness. The return walls of the north and south towers are supported from the aisle walls with buttresses that have diminished arcading.

During the nineteenth-century restoration many of the Purbeck marble shafts were renewed with Ashburton, a stone that weathers to a different colour and has changed the appearance of many parts of the cathedral, including the west front.

Scott used Redfern as sculptor for the statues but many of them were produced in Salisbury in the workshop of William Osmond who, together with his father, was connected with masonry work at the cathedral from 1818 until 1880. There are some true Redfern statues, with carving of a different class. The Osmond statues tend to have features that look similar and pantograph holes can be traced where measurements were transferred from the model to the block of stone.

### The North Porch

The north porch was no doubt intended to be the main

entrance to the cathedral and as such is enriched with detail. The north arch is set on Purbeck shafted jambs with moulded bases and heads. In the seventeenth century this arch was filled with a wooden screen with double doors. Inside, the east and west walls have two tiers of arcading, the lower rising on Purbeck shafts from the wall plinth, the upper arcading being of two orders standing on a ledge formed by the thinning of the wall thickness. The tracery is similar to that at triforium within the cathedral. The south wall is pierced by a double arched opening with cusped inner order of moulding. Above the opening within a quatrefoil set in a vesica is a figure of Christ in Glory. The vaulting is similar to that of the nave aisles, and the outer walls of the porch resemble those of the aisles but without windows.

The interior of the porch was restored in 1880 under the direction of G. E. Street. The doors with their elaborate hinges, the entrance gates, boot scraper and chandelier are all part of Street's work.

### The Parvis Room

Above the north arch of the porch is a pair of windows that light the first floor Parvis Room. The upper storey has served many functions; it was the only such room when the cathedral was first consecrated in 1258 and may well have been used as a repository for manuscripts. It has also served as a retreat for sextons and nightwatchmen. There is a fireplace with a hearth set some four feet (120 cm) above the floor, with a stone flue that emerges on the east side of the roof. When the fireplace was opened up in 1986 several clay pipes were found at the back of the hearth, no doubt from clandestine smoking by those on duty.

The roof timbers, which are original, are exposed to the Parvis Room, the construction being of trussed rafters with scissor bracing and collars. There is a double wallplate, the rafters landing on the outer and ashlar to the inner.

The roof joins that of the aisle and is one of only four sections of original timber roof left in the cathedral. On the south wall of the Parvis Room is a section of original painted decoration. It is stencilled and seems to be a standard pattern that was used elsewhere in the cathedral. The inner walls are of rubble and the vaulting of the porch is filled to form the floor. At present the room holds a small permanent exhibition of artefacts and items of interest.

## The Nave

The nave exterior is simple in design with each bay of the aisle wall having a two-light window and the bays divided by buttresses of four orders. The triforium and clerestory parapets are decorated with trefoil headed arcading below which is a tabling course of trefoil arches supported on foliated corbels. A feature of the aisle walls is the horizontal moulding courses at ground and sill levels and weathering to the buttresses. The clerestory is supported within the aisle roofs by flying buttresses that land against the tas de charge. No buttresses were visible on the exterior until after the completion of the tower and spire. Where external flyers were built in the fourteenth and fifteenth centuries the internal ones were demolished. Each clerestory bay has a triple light window, the bays are divided with pilaster type buttresses and, in places, flying buttresses. These are of two types indicating the period in which they were built.

## The Roof

The nave roof is of double queen post trusses, with purlins, rafters and wind bracing, all dating from the sixteenth century. In its reconstruction a great deal of the original timber was re-used, resulting in there being mortice holes in rafters for no apparent reason.

The south aisle roof is eighteenth-century, part of the work having been undertaken by Francis Price. The north aisle roof is still in its original form, consisting of two half trusses in each bay fixed between the internal buttresses. Some of the roof boarding is of cleft oak dating from the early seventeenth century, as is some of the leadwork at the west end of this aisle.

## The North Transept

The north end of the north transept is of four storeys each with glazing. Two main and two secondary buttresses divide the face vertically. The upper window lights the roof space which is eighteenth-century in structure. A stairway is contained in the north-west corner giving access to all levels. The pinnacles at the gable of the transept and on the end of the aisle are all different, matched only by those on the end of the south transept. The aisle walls match those of the nave, and flying buttresses divide each bay of the clerestory. In the centre of the transept wall was a doorway until the end of the eighteenth century. On the outside was a porch that presumably came

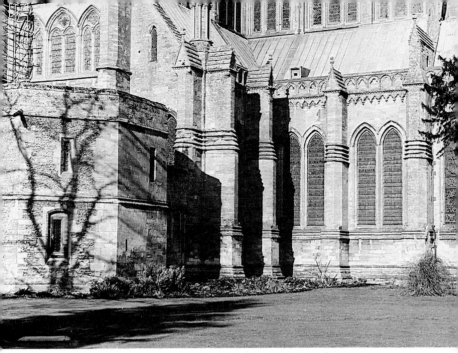

*The former treasury and muniment room (left) with the south face of the presbytery where a verger's house once stood.*

from elsewhere. Its style matches nothing that can be found at the cathedral and it now stands in the grounds of the Council offices in Salisbury.

The porch was purchased in 1790 by Henry Penruddoche Wyndham. He removed it to the grounds of his house, now the Council offices, placed on it a plaque declaring that it had originally been constructed at Old Sarum and had been moved to the new City 'where, for upwards of five hundred years, it served as a Vestibule to the Northern Door of the Cathedral'. On the inside of the transept the tomb of Bishop Blyth covers the outline of the doorway.

### The Eastern End

The eastern transepts again have four storeys but a different arrangement of windows. The eastern roofs at high level are of the eighteenth century except the north-east transept where the structure is original. It consists of trussed rafter construction, each truss having a scissor brace and collar. The aisles have no visible buttresses, nor does the clerestory of the presbytery. The eastern gable of the presbytery has a five-light window lighting the roof space, below which is a three-light window with a blank arch on either side. This window was lowered in

1781 to accommodate the 'Moses' glass, the sill level being lowered by some two feet (60 cm), presumably to give better proportions to the design of the glass. The gable is buttressed on either side, the buttresses being of the fifteenth century.

The east walls of the choir aisles have three–light windows in their gables lighting the roof spaces. Both the north and south sections of roofing are original, similar in construction to the north–east transept and north porch.

The east wall of the Trinity Chapel is where the foundation stones were laid in 1220. The face is divided vertically into three sections by buttresses, each section having a gabled finish. In the central gable a three-light window is flanked by niches with plinths intended to receive sculptures. The window lights the roof space that was for many years the glaziers' shop.

On the plinth of the outer buttresses and below the central light of the lower window are consecration crosses. In their centres can be seen the fixing places for holding bronze or brass crosses. The crosses mark the various places where the new cathedral was blessed during the consecration of 1258. On either side of the Trinity Chapel stood the chantries of Hungerford and Beauchamp. There is little visible evidence to show where they once stood.

Against the south wall of the presbytery stood a verger's house and St Stephen's porch. Both were cleared away during Wyatt's work. The entrance to the aisle can still be traced. There is a step at the base of the wall and the outline of the infilled doorway can be seen. On the eastern buttress of the south aisle of the presbytery are two shallow cut niches. One is now filled with stone and one partly with mortar. To the side of the niches is cut an inscription, an indulgence for thirteen days for an unknown person. There is a further inscription low down on the east face of the buttress. A. R. Malden, in a paper presented in 1906, suggests it is a memorial to Adam Mottram, Precentor of Salisbury from 1397–1415.

Attached to the south-east transept is the vestry and choir practice room, formerly the treasury and muniment room. The outer walls are of stone ashlars on the east side but of flintwork with stone dressings on the other sides, one of only two examples of such walling in the cathedral.

## The South Transept

The south transept is the same in form as the north transept. Its roof, constructed in the same manner as the nave, dates from

*The south side of the Trinity Chapel, the site of the Beauchamp Chapel, now a burial garth.*

*The Chapter House, with a mulberry tree to the left.*

the sixteenth century. In the central bay of the south wall there was originally a porch, which had been removed before Wyatt's work of the eighteenth century.

The section of cloister from the south transept to the Chapter House vestibule is of two storeys, the upper one being the library. In the wall below is a doorway which was the processional way from the cathedral to the canons' graveyard.

## The Chapter House

The Chapter House has the same mouldings to plinth, sill and buttresses as the rest of the cathedral. From each angle of the parapet come grotesque water spouts. The roof is supported by an octagonal central post which is original and has a moulded base. On this rest eight beams fixed at their other ends into the angles of the building. Raking pieces from the underside of the beams to the central post give it the look of a great umbrella. The main beams are some 40 feet (12.2 metres) long and 12 inches by 10 inches (30 cm by 25 cm) in section. In 1971–72 five of them were renewed.

The south wall of the cloister is of flint and stone rubble. It contains fragments from Old Sarum and in the eastern bay a new doorway has been cut, only the second new doorway since the building of the cathedral. The cloister parapet is of the same pattern as triforium and clerestory and the bays are marked by buttresses. A careful examination of the west cloister wall will reveal areas where small rounded chips of stone have been removed. When King's House was occupied during the Civil War the soldiers used the west wall of the churchyard on which to rest their muskets, firing at the cloister wall where their musket balls removed the rounded chips. Undoubtedly, the statues on the west front also came under fire!

There is a simple grandeur to the exterior of Salisbury and, enhanced by its surroundings, it is possibly remembered by more people than is the interior.

W. H. Hudson, revisiting Salisbury, describes the exterior with its colouring of nature and although a non-believer, remarked: 'One marvels at a building so vast in size which yet produces the effect of a palace in fairyland, or of a cathedral not built with hands but brought into existence by a miracle.

I began to think it not safe to stay in that place too long, lest it should compel me to stay there always, or cause me to feel dissatisfied and homesick when away.'

47

## Chapter Three

# THE
# TOWER AND SPIRE

THE CROWNING GLORY of Salisbury is its tower and spire, a feature long remembered by those who visit the cathedral, and one constantly in the view of those who live and work in and around Salisbury. From the early fourteenth century the spire became a landmark by which travellers set course to the new city of Sarum, changing the direction of roads and tracks. The tower and spire rise some 290 feet (88 metres) above the ridge of the main roofs, a total of 404 feet (123 metres) from ground level. Although in a valley, the spire is visible at times from a distance of some 18 miles (28 km) to the west, where the A303 begins its descent into Mere.

It is difficult to imagine the cathedral without the tower and spire or even with only a tower. This indicates the original artist's intention to have something more than just a low lantern against which the main roof rested. The designer who laid plans for the work in the 1280s, may well have been Robert the Mason, who saw the completion of the rest of the cathedral.

As mentioned previously, there is strong evidence to suggest a building date of 1280–1320. Certainly the work was finished by 1328. After this, Chapter records are virtually complete and do not contain any reference to the work. The evidence of the architecture also confirms that the difference between the west front and the tower is not of any great period of time. The ballflowers around the west window of the nave and the lozenge pattern moulding on the west front are matched on the tower, with differences that show the logical development of detail and design. We may never know for certain who the master mason was but what he left is a superb piece of stone engineering.

*The Tower*

From approximately 1240 until the commencement of the tower, the lantern stage was open to the cathedral below. In each angle of the lantern were two single lancet windows, the outline of which can still be seen. The lancets would have given sufficient light only to enhance the interior of the lantern, showing up the arcading of Purbeck shafts and detached piers. A walkway at the base of the arcading gave access to doors leading into roof spaces. The lantern may well have been capped with either a flat or a low pyramidal roof. On the exterior there is shallow blank arcading, diminishing in height to correspond with the slope of the roofs. A tabling course, seen from inside the roofs, shows that the present roof construction follows the original roof line. The tabling course is grooved on its top edge to form a run-off for any water that entered the joint between the roofs and walls of the tower. The top of the lantern was finished with a crenellated parapet with two water spouts on each face.

During the extension of the tower, the lantern or stage one of the tower underwent several changes. To form a 'foundation' for the work, the upper section of the walls were demolished as far as the string course below the crenellations on the outer face and to the top of the arcading on the inner face. The present crenellations are not original but part of the late thirteenth-century work done to maintain the original line of the lantern roof. The remains of the water spouts appear some two courses lower, indicating the level to which the exterior masonry was dismantled. Inside the lantern the late thirteenth-century masonry can be distinguished from that of the middle of the century.

To cut off the work from the cathedral below, a wooden floor was built using some of the original roof beams of the lantern. These were covered on their underside with tongued and grooved boarding to form a ceiling. During repairs to the floor in 1971, remains of the boarding were rediscovered, showing that the boarding had been sawn from between the beams when the vaulting beneath was built in 1479.

As the work of extending the tower progressed, the space between the piers of the arcade and the rear wall were filled to form points of stiffening. Iron bands were fitted to the base of the piers and secured into the walls behind. At the top of the arcade iron bracing was fitted to prevent any outward movement. This ironwork was fitted at a later date, possibly about

*Iron bracing within the lantern stage of the tower.*

1300, using in some cases the putlog-holes of scaffolding to connect the internal and external sections of the frame. The iron bars used are approximately two inches (5 cm) square and are formed into a frame that runs around the inner face of the lantern with cross bars joining opposite sides. Vertical bars are joined to the cross bracing by curved struts with cusping. Wren described this frame as possibly the finest ironwork of its age in Europe. Bolts of two inch (5 cm) diameter join the inner band to an outer band that encompasses the lantern immediately below the ballflower string course. The exterior ironwork was protected by sheet lead flashing and when uncovered in 1974 was found to be in excellent condition.

Inside the roofs abutting the corners of the lantern are short flying buttresses that appear to be original. There are two at each corner and are part of a system of forty-four buttresses built to protect and relieve the weight from the first stage of the tower. Below the floor is a band of ironwork dating from

*The north-west angle of the tower. The crenellations mark the junction of the buttress and pinnacle. A seventeenth-century iron band encircles the buttress.*

51

1740 and jointed according to instructions in Wren's note-book. A template in yellow deal was made and the iron forged by Richard Pearce at Romsey. This ironwork runs round the base of the lantern stage and encompasses the corner turrets. On the outside of the turrets the ironwork is protected with lead flashing. Francis Price shows a drawing of this ironwork in his book. The stairways in the lantern section were filled with brickwork between 1936 and 1939 as a precaution against pressure caused by the Shields's nineteenth-century iron brac-ings.

Shields was appointed consulting engineer by the Dean and Chapter after Scott voiced his concern about the stability of the lantern stage. Shields's diagonal bracing was to have been part of a larger scheme of reinforcing work that was to have included a system of bracing in the arcade. Some further form of reinforcing is again being planned at present.

The cross bracing is of iron but is joined and tightened by a system of folding wedges as if it were of timber. It is also wrapped in hair-felt to prevent condensation forming on the cold iron.

The second stage of the tower, begun by 1285, has a course of crenellations and one of ballflowers joined by intertwining stems as a base. Octagonal corner turrets contain stairways, and the corner masonry is decorated with arcaded panelling divided by pilaster buttresses. In the two central divisions of the buttresses are two-light windows with trefoil heads with a cinquefoil recessed panel above. Each window is finished with a crocketed gable with a foliated finial. The outer divisions have a blank recess formed in exactly the same way as the windows. The mullions and jambs are decorated with ball-flowers, some two hundred and eighty around each window or recess. Horizontal banding of quatrefoil panels is placed halfway up the windows.

Separating stage two from stage three is a heavily moulded course with a base of roll moulding and ballflowers topped with a course of triangular panels each inset with a trefoil recess. The top section has an open V at the base of which are carved animal heads similar to German Shepherd dogs. Each panel in the upper section has a foliated finial. At the base of each gable over the pilasters are carved small animal heads that look like poodles, which can only be seen in detail when hanging over the side of the tower in a bosun's chair!

Stage three of the tower has variations. It is smaller in size,

*Animal heads forming part of the decoration on the tower.*

*The junction of the spire and the tower on the south side of the cathedral.*

forming a slight setback in the outer wall. The windows and recesses are the same but the gable finishes are different. Inside the windows extra mullions were built to help relieve weight from the arches above. This stage is capped with a string course of ballflowers and a lozenge panelled parapet topped with foliated finials. The corner turrets are finished with spirelets with crocketed angles. Behind these are pinnacles that fill the space between the face of the spire and the corner of the tower and help to support the squinch arches. Each cardinal face of the spire has two doorways giving the name by which this level is called, 'eight doors'.

## The Spire

The spire is octagonal with a roll moulding at each angle. The moulding has a decoration of ballflowers placed either side of it up to the first band of panel work. Above this level the angle moulding has crockets. There are three bands of lozenge panel decoration, each panel having a quatrefoil recess. The bands are framed at top and bottom with double rows of ballflowers.

At the top of the spire is an octagonal capstone surmounted by a metal cross. From the top of the tower to the top of the spire is 180 feet (54.86 metres). For 20 feet (6.96 metres) the walls are approximately 2 feet (60 cm) thick; above this point the walls reduce to 8 inches (20 cm). The panelled decoration is cut back into the 8 inch (20 cm) thickness leaving no more than 2 to 3 inches (5 cm to 7.5 cm) of stone in the centre of the quatrefoils. Most of the stones in the spire are cramped to each other horizontally with iron cramps fixed into the stones with lead, forming each course into a reinforced ring.

A spire is a difficult structure to build unless the initial planning is done well. The easy way is to draw one face of the spire full size so that courses can be determined, angled plumb rules made, moulds made for the panelled decoration and measuring rods made to gauge the progress of the work. The nave floor is of sufficient size for such a layout to have been made.

Inside the first stage of tower is the cathedral clock, installed in 1884 by members of the 62nd Wiltshire Regiment as a memorial to their comrades who died in India and Aden between 1868 and 1882. The clock was built by J. B. Joyce and Co. of Whitchurch in Shropshire. The clock is connected to bells hanging in the third stage of the tower. There are four quarter bells, cast in 1884 by Taylors of Loughborough and an hour bell that is a survivor from the detached bell tower. It was recast in 1661 to commemorate Charles II's restoration to the throne. Its weight is 28 hundredweight (1,422 kg) and it was removed from the bell tower in 1790 along with the four-teenth-century clock that now stands in the nave.

The third stage of tower contains a wooden framework that forms a reinforcing to the base of the original scaffolding within the spire. A series of vertical posts with cross bracing connect beams built into the tower wall at floor level and beams at the base of the spire. In the south-west corner is a strut that has been strengthened by timber being fixed either side of damage caused by fire. This is the only visible evidence of the fire of 1742 when on 21 June lightning struck the west face of the tower. Early next morning the head verger saw smoke pouring out of the windows and raised the alarm. In his book Francis Price, who was clerk of the works at the time, describes the fire as 'roaring like that when the baker is preparing his oven for the bread'. A chain of people was organized and the fire put out. The charred strut was left as a reminder by Price as to what might have happened but, as he says, 'the noble structure was not yet near its end'. Other instances of lightning strikes are 1431 'the spire of Our Lady Church set on fire by lightning', and 1641 when again lightning was the cause. The first lightning conductor was fitted to the spire some time at the beginning of the nineteenth century. In 1850 scaffolding was erected to renew the lightning conductor. Again in 1903 the conductor on the spire was renewed and the whole of the cathedral given protection. At that time it was the longest lightning conductor system in the world.

Inside the spire is a wooden framework that formed the scaffolding from which the spire was built. It is easier to build from the inside than it is to erect external scaffolding on a sloping building. There are three stages of square framing with a central post. Above this the central post has a series of 'floors' consisting of horizontal members radiating from it, these members having struts back to the post looking like the ribs of an umbrella.

The frame would have been extended above the level of the work to provide some form of temporary roof cover. This may well have occurred at each of the 'floors'. The frame then was a mixture of scaffolding, support for a temporary roof, a means of access, a support from which further supports could be fixed to hold each course of masonry until it was finished, and finally it was used to tension the structure. The central post at its uppermost end was joined to the base of the rod coming through the capstone from the cross. With a special arrangement of iron brackets and folding wedges the whole of the spire could be tensioned, a system of tensioning that, with variations after the work in 1949–51, still remains. When conditions demand it, the spire can still be 'tightened up'.

The interior scaffolding was of little use for the building of the last fifty feet (15 metres) of the spire. Some 10 feet (3 metres) below the sill of the weather door holes were left in the walls through which passed the supports for an external scaffolding from which the upper part could be finished. When the scaffold was dismantled (c.1320) the holes in the walls were fitted with stones in which iron handles had been fixed, so that in the future the stones could easily be removed when scaffolding was needed again.

Approximately 80 per cent of the timber inside the spire is original and through the centre of the framework are ten wooden ladders that allow access up to the weather door. This is a small opening on the north face of the spire some 40 feet (12 metres) below the capstone. From this point the route to the top of the spire is on the outside. When the weather door is opened the view is across the city towards Old Sarum and 360 feet (110 metres) to ground level. Rungs are built into the masonry either side one of the angles of the spire. The lower rungs are of iron encased in lead, just large enough on which to fit the toe of a boot. The climb up the final 40 feet (12 metres) is like that at the top of an extremely tall pole where one can see around both sides. At the capstone the outward bulge makes it awkward to lean back and reach for handgrips at the same time. The haul round the capstone is rewarded with the sensation of being cast adrift on a small raft of stone floating 404 feet (123 m) above ground level.

Colonel John Wyndham in 1684 measured the height of the spire using a barometer. His experiment was recorded thus by Francis Price: 'the height of the weather-cock of Our Lady's church at Salisbury, from the ground is 4280 inches. The mercury subsided in that height 42/100 of an inch.' He affirmed that 'the height of the said steeple is four hundred and four feet, which he hath tried several times, and found always to answer exactly'.

Wyndham also laid out the Meridian mark on the north wall of the churchyard. Using the spire as the gnomon of a giant sundial, the shadow of the spire points towards the mark at mid-day.

At the base of the spire is a windlass that has kept its original form although it has been repaired many times. It is intended to be pulled round from the outer rim, where four men can grasp hand-holds. The maximum lift is nearly a ton. By this method stone was raised from ground level when the spire was being built.

There are many stories connected with the spire and tales of those who have climbed to the top. In 1665 the cathedral plumber, known as 'Old Haley', climbed to the capstone and roasted 'a shoulder of mutton and a couple of fowls upon the top of Our Lady spire'. There is no record of what he did with the meat when it was cooked!

King Charles II came to Salisbury in 1665 and amongst other activities climbed to the top of the tower to see the view of the city. An account of this records 'Two boys fell from the eight doors, and pitching upon the leads of the church, were killed'. On another visit by Charles II to the cathedral, a sailor climbed to the top of the spire where he stood on his head! The king refused to give him any money because he did not wish to encourage such foolhardiness.

Francis Price writes in 1747 of another custom concerning the Whitsun fair that was held in the Close, when sometimes as many as eight or ten persons at a time climbed to the top of the spire. 'The late Bishop, dean and chapter, put a stop to these fool-hardy practices, by which many lives were hazarded without the least advantage to those who attempted it: and the danger was the greater because these people never went up but when heated with liquor, which furnished them with that unnecessary courage. It seems they had certain sports in their passage up and down, viz. those who were the highest had the pleasure of discharging urine on those below!' He then points out the damage that can be done to lead and stone by the effects of urine and that it must 'hasten the natural decays'.

When the capstone was built it is said that a container was placed inside it holding a fragment of the Virgin's shroud. In the late seventeenth century iron reinforcing was placed around the capstone, the casket was found and contained a piece of cloth. In 1762, when a new vane was placed on the spire, the workmen discovered the casket again, in a cavity on the south side of the capstone. It consisted of a lead container within which was a wooden one. Inside this were 'remains of a

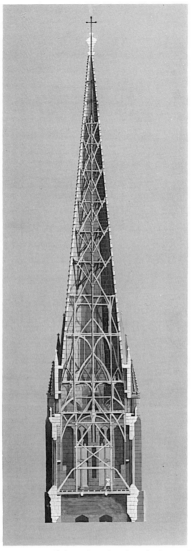

*Cecil Hewitt's painting of the spire, showing the internal woodwork.*

piece of silk or fine linin cloth, so much decayed as to have only the appearance of tinder'. The casket was removed again in 1849 and replaced inside one made of copper. When the top 23 feet (7 m) of the spire were rebuilt in 1949–51 the casket was removed and placed in the cathedral library. Its place was taken

59

by a copper scroll inside a copper container giving details of the work and the people concerned with it. Unfortunately, it does not record the names of the men who did the work, only the Bishop, Dean and Chapter, the architect and the contractors.

At the corners of the lantern stage are fourteenth-century flying buttresses that rise from the aisle walls. The tops of the buttresses are encompassed by the nineteenth-century iron-work designed by Shields. Wren suggested further buttresses against the corners of the lantern and on the south-west corner a start was made on building two of them. A foundation was placed on the main walls of nave and south transept, and the vertical stiffener and upper landing point were built but no flyer. The extra masonry gives the corner a bulky appearance and had the project been completed would have spoiled the look of the junction of tower with the roofs.

When looking at the tower and spire its foundations and lower supports must also be considered, especially in view of the weight carried by the foundations. Above the original lantern stage is something in the order of 6,400 tons (6,500 tonnes) of extra building materials. This was placed on an area ill designed to take such weight. The whole of the central weight of the cathedral is carried on four main piers whose foundations go barely 4 feet (1.2 metres) into the ground. Below the cathedral is a natural layer of flint gravel brought there by the rivers that flow into the valley. The layer of gravel is firm and provided a raft-like foundation for the cathedral. Beneath the central area the layer of gravel extends downwards for some 27 feet (8.2 metres), sufficient to ensure that equilibrium is maintained between the thrust of the piers and the resistance of the gravel. However, it needs little to cause this equilibrium to become disturbed.

The original builders created a fine and elegant structure and the best place to consider its merits is from the top of the spire. When the wind is gusting at the right frequency, movement can be felt on top of the capstone which serves as a reminder that it was designed and built without the aid of present hindsight and knowledge, yet has still stood against the ravages of time. At the present time (1986) work has started that will ensure the future safety of the spire.

## Chapter Four

# THE INTERIOR

W ITH ITS OPEN and uncluttered interior Salisbury Cathedral has a simple unity, its various parts all being brought together in the vista from west to east. There is great beauty in its simplicity and in the geometric perfection of the design. It matters little if some have remarked that the triforium is not tall enough, it cannot now be altered any more than any of the supposed defects, so enjoy what is seen. Imagine the amount of effort needed to create the cathedral during its thirty-eight-year building period. Effort by labourers, masons, carpenters, plumbers and glaziers brought to fruition what Bishop Poore initiated.

From the west end of the nave the whole length of the cathedral is in view. Even when the screen and pulpitum were in position, at the west end of the choir, it would still have been possible to follow the line of the high vault and see the lower vaulting of the Trinity Chapel terminating against the eastern wall. The present 'open' view is the result of changes in fashion, changes in the way the cathedral has been used, a view achieved by the removal of 'furnishings' and not alteration to the structure. As seen today, the structure of the interior differs little from the late thirteenth century, any differences being small additions to help with the support of the tower and spire.

The best place to view the interior is from the walkway under the west window of the nave. During summer months visitors are sometimes taken in guided groups past this point. At this level the arcade, triforium and clerestory are seen to better advantage. Beneath the triforium arcade is a Purbeck marble string course which, near to the central crossing, bends downwards from the horizontal. This deflection is one of the

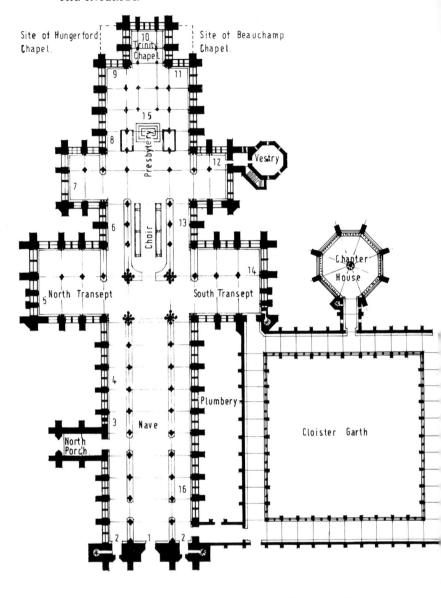

St Mary's Cathedral Church.        Ground Plan.
SALISBURY.

results of adding the tower and spire, causing the centre of the cathedral to sink, or settle, some 7 inches (18 cm). It is, however, the symmetry of the interior that attracts the eye.

### The Nave

The main arcading of the nave is of ten bays with arches and piers that are all the same. Each arch has the same mouldings, as has each capital and base of the piers. Below triforium level the only small difference in each bay is in the carvings of the label stops and even these are all of foliage.

The piers stand on a raised plinth, which forms part of the foundation, as does the benching at the base of the aisle walls. The foundations of the cathedral are of flint, chalk, stone and lime mortar resting on a natural layer of flint gravel. Beneath the outer walls and the arcading are strip foundations that are only slightly wider than the walls or the piers. There are also cross foundations or ground beams running north and south between aisle wall and piers and from pier to pier. The worked masonry of the walls starts one foot (30 cm) below floor level.

The piers are quatrefoil in plan and are of unpolished Purbeck laid on its natural bed. Around each pier are four detached polished Purbeck shafts where the bed of the stone runs vertically. The sections of shafting are connected with bronze rings that cover the joints.

The bases and capitals are moulded and follow the outline of pier and shafts. Each bay of the triforium arcade has two main divisions which in turn have two sub-divisions. There is a rear relieving arch to each bay, the jambs have shaft clusters and the intermediate supports are clusters of Purbeck shafts. Each bay is basically the same but alternate bays have repeat changes in the tracery. The clerestory arcade is formed by the outline of the vaulting which rises from Purbeck shafts resting on corbel heads. Within this outline are three moulded arches that match the lancets of the windows. The arches are supported by two free-standing clusters of shafts with collars. A walkway runs at the base of the clerestory but is blocked at the east end of the nave by reinforcing work done after the building of the tower and spire. The vaulting is of Chilmark arches and ribs with an infill of 9 inches (22.5 cm) of tufa covered with 6 inches (15 cm) of lime concrete; on the underside of the panels are two coats of lime plaster.

The aisle windows have splayed jambs, mullions and sills. The jambs have double shafts and the mullions a single one, the shafts being collared. From the wall benching of the aisles rise Purbeck shafts from whose tops rises the vaulting. On the arcade side of the aisles the vault rises from the piers.

Only two bays of the nave aisles have any differences: the westernmost on the south side, where the lower part of the windows are filled in to accommodate the west walk of the cloister. Here also is a doorway leading into the cloister. The fifth bay from the west on the north side has the entrance leading from the north porch.

The west wall of the nave has a large three-light window in front of which is an arcade with free-standing shafts of Purbeck. Below the window is an arcaded gallery of four bays, each bay of two openings having shafted jambs. This gallery has in its rear wall quatrefoil openings now filled with stone but, at one time, open (see p. 36). The gallery is approached by steps leading from walkways under the west windows of the aisles from where access is available to the stairways at the north and south ends of the west front. Below the gallery is the west door, in the centre of a three-arch blind arcade. The doorway is double arched and the wooden doors with cross bracing are original. They were repaired in the eighteenth century when infills were placed between the bracing to prevent draughts coming through the outer boarding. The fine brass lock dates from the eighteenth century and has the Radnor crest on it, suggesting it came from Longford Castle. In addition to the lock there is a wooden bar that fits into holes in the door jambs. One hole is deep enough to allow the bar to slide into it. This must have been a feature planned when the wall was built. The sill of the west window and that of the gallery do not match those of the clerestory or triforium. They are connected by vertical mouldings, the reason being the separation of the west front horizontally at different levels to the rest of the cathedral. Although an oddity it blends very well.

In the spandrels of the west window can be seen a date of 1620 painted on the wall; a date of 1622 appears on the wall in the spandrel of the easternmost clerestory window on the north side of the nave. There was work carried out in the early seventeenth century and Dodsworth used this knowledge to claim that the red masonry lines were painted on the vaulting at this time. The paint lines, however, are contemporary with

*The west wall of the nave.*

the building of the vaulting. The vaulting of the aisles may not have been built until after the completion of the nave because in the north aisle roof the wall plate is decorated with arcading which would have been for the benefit of those looking from below. There is no evidence of this on the south side as the roof was renewed in the eighteenth century.

One thing that escapes most people's imagination is how the interior originally looked after dark. Candles and torches would have lit only fragmented areas, throwing flickering shadows. In the nineteenth century gas lighting was installed, fishtail burners coming from a pipe that ran along the edge of the triforium in a groove cut into the Purbeck marble. Vergers had to climb around the triforium holding a lighted taper, turn on taps and light the burners. The first electric lights were installed in 1910 when five lights, the main and secondary wiring and main switch cost £40. The present lighting in the nave was a gift of The Friends of Salisbury Cathedral in 1984. It reveals the architecture in a way that the original builders could only imagine. On occasion the interior is still lit by candles which, for a brief period, give something of the mystery and beauty that such light gives to the cathedral.

## The North Aisle

In the north aisle is the fourteenth-century clock that was originally in the detached bell tower and moved to the tower of the cathedral in the eighteenth century. When the present cathedral clock was installed in 1884 the old clock was dismantled and stored in the roof of the north transept. In 1956 The Friends of the Cathedral paid for the restoration of the clock to a working condition. The frame is constructed of iron but the jointing is done as if it were of wood with wedged mortise and tenon joints. It is the oldest existing clock in England and possibly the earliest remaining mechanical clock in virtually complete and working condition in the world.

The clock was made in or before 1386 as the cathedral accounts for that year show that a provision was made for funds to maintain a clock. There are similarities with the Wells clock, now in the Science Museum, particularly in details of the frame and escape mechanism. Bishop Erghum was at Salisbury when the clock was made in 1386, moved to Wells in 1388 and four years later the Wells clock was made. This ancient timepiece has, during its working life, ticked in excess of 500,000,000 times.

*The fourteenth-century clock, the oldest still working in Europe.*

Near the clock hang Regimental Colours of the Wiltshire Regiment and the Duke of Edinburgh's Regiment. Here, too, is the bell of *H.M.S Salisbury* with, inside the bell, the names of crew members' babies christened on board the ship.

The interior wooden draught lobby over the entrance from the north porch has engraved glass in the panels flanking the doors. These panels are the work of Laurence Whistler with scenes from the Dorset countryside and a quotation from T. S. Eliot. They are in memory of Joanna and Serena, the sisters of Christopher Booker.

At the east end of the south aisle is a floor slab covering the ashes of Sir Arthur Bryant. The simple inscription, 'Historian of his country', tells more than a thousand words.

At the west end of the north aisle is a diocesan map showing all the parishes. It was presented to the Dean and Chapter by young people of the diocese to commemorate the seven hundredth anniversary of the consecration of the cathedral in 1958. Next to the map is a slate slab with the names of all the Bishops of Salisbury to date cut into the surface. Either side of the slab can be seen the inner mouldings of door jambs. There was a doorway here to give access to the cloister which was blocked when the west walk of the cloister was built one bay further west than was planned.

The nave has been subject to flooding at times, on which occasions the clergy were known to ride into the cathedral to keep their feet dry. There is a photograph of the last occasion, 1915, and to commemorate the event a brass marker plate was fixed on the base of the wall benching at the east end of the north aisle.

## The Central Crossing

The area is bounded by the four main piers that support the greater part of the weight of the tower and spire. Above the vaulting rises the tower and spire, terminating 404 feet (123 m) above the pavement.

To see the effect that the extra weight of the tower and spire has had, look up any one of the piers and see how far they have bent. The bending is due to the piers being forced outwards by the thrust of the arches. In the triforium and clerestory, at the angles where transepts, choir and nave meet, can be seen flying buttresses that were built to help contain the movement of the arches. At triforium there are two buttresses and at clerestory, one. There is a look of haste about the construction of some of the buttresses, as if there was not time to secure the individual stones in a proper manner. In two cases stones have slipped and then been trapped by the movement. Certain of the clerestory windows that abut the piers were filled in as a further means of strengthening.

Over the centuries there has been concern about the possibility of continuing movement in the piers, either by sinking or bending. In the first half of the fifteenth century bracing arches were built to the north and south sides of the crossing to help restrain any tendency of the piers to continue bending. The treatment would have been more effective had similar arches been built on the east and west sides, forming a complete girdle of restraint. This was done at Wells but using a different form of arched support. The two that were built were placed against the piers, the detached shafting having been first removed. The arches have piers of their own, the eastern ones originally resting partly on the thirteenth-century pulpitum. When this was moved in the eighteenth century the bottoms of the piers had to be made good to floor level onto new

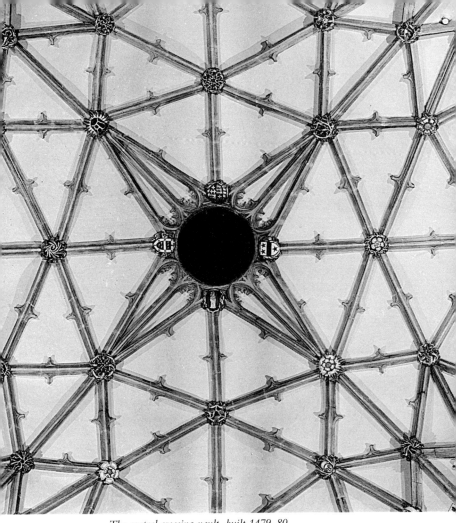

*The central crossing vault, built 1479–80.*

foundations. The arches terminate with a battlemented top just above the sill line of triforium.

In the spandrels are trefoil-headed openings, forming a diminishing arcade set within square-headed panels of moulding outlined with florets. Beneath the battlemented top is a cornice of carved heads and foliage, the heads including a king, a bishop, a wood spirit and grotesques. Each side of the arch piers are canopied niches, six of which contain statues. The statues were placed as memorials to those named on the base of each one. The figures on the south side of the south arch represent Elias de Dereham (west end) shown with set-square and compasses. At the east end is Bishop Poore with a model of the cathedral.

Above the crossing is a vaulting built 1479–80 under the direction of John Spyring the clerk of the works. The ribs are of Haselbury stone, from near Bath, and the panelling infill of chalk with the underside plastered. The vault is decorated with carved bosses of foliage and one head, that of The Green Man or wood spirit, with foliage coming from his mouth. The vault was redecorated in 1970 at which time gold replaced the previous yellow ochre paint of the seventeenth century. Seventeenth-century dates found in the nave and other areas indicate that work was done at high level. In decorating the crossing vault no gold leaf was used and the seventeenth-century painter appears to have had little faith in the support he was standing on for he splashed paint onto the ribs and panels in his haste to get the work finished. Beneath the seventeenth-century paint traces of gold leaf were found but no former descriptive decoration could be seen on the four shields around the central hole. Here were painted arms appropriate to the fifteenth century. To the west, the Royal arms of the period, to the east, the arms of the cathedral, to the north those of Bishop Beauchamp and to the south those of Bishop Poore.

In the corner of the vaulting are shields of hardboard with a representation of what could be seen of the original paintings that are now covered with the new shields. The original paintings are done directly onto the plaster infilling, outline drawings made with a sharp instrument scratching the surface of the plaster. In the south-east corner are the five wounds that Christ suffered and the instruments of the Passion. In the north-east corner are the arms of Hugh Pavy, a canon of the cathedral who became Bishop of St Davids.

The pulpit was designed by Sir Gilbert Scott and the work done by Farmer and Brindley of London. The base and supporting shafting are of Purbeck marble, the body is Chilmark with Purbeck insets. On each face figures stand in niches formed by recesses. They represent Noah, Elijah, Jonah, St John the Baptist, St Peter and St Paul. The steps are of Chilmark and the handrail and balustrading by Skidmore of Coventry.

Skidmore's screen, which formed the western entrance to the choir, was removed one night in 1959 by order of the Dean and Chapter. From his Coventry workshops Skidmore produced a series of screens of which only Lichfield's and Hereford's remain. Salisbury's was erected to the memory of Dean Lear, whose widow would not accept Scott's idea for a stone screen and insisted that if £1,000 could produce a screen at Lichfield or Hereford then that was all she was spending. Scott's original idea was to produce a screen based on a design influenced by the thirteenth-century pulpitum.

Over the years since the building of the tower and spire there have been periods during which measurements have been taken to check the movement, if any, of the structure. Wren carried out his plumbing and calculations and soon afterwards Thomas Naish did the same. In 1737 another Thomas Naish, son of the first one, together with Francis Price, carried out a series of measurements. A plumb line was dropped from the sill of the weather door, 40 feet (12 m) from the top of the spire, to the pavement of the crossing. Here a mark was made to show where the plumb bob rested, an octagon was marked on the floor showing the interior size of the spire at the point where the plumb line was hanging. To have a relating mark, the centre of each side of the crossing was found and lines run through converging on where the brass plate marked 'centre of the tower' is fixed. The difference between this plate and the centre of the octagon is the amount of declination in the first 360 feet (109 m) of the tower and spire. Bishop Sherlock either didn't trust the clerk of the works, or wanted another opinion, and asked Mr Mill of London to check the measurements. A line was placed down the centre of the cathedral and run out to the western boundary of the churchyard. Here Mr Mill erected a frame from which hung a plumb line directly over the line. On an opposite axis, north-south, a lighted candle was moved until flame and capstone of the spire lined up with the plumb line.

Mr Mill carried out the same procedure on a north-south line, thus finding the declination of the spire to the south and the west. His measurements agreed with those of Naish and Bishop Sherlock asked for them to be recorded on a floor slab having its own foundation.

The floor slab has an inset of darker stone in one corner. This is where the present cross hit the floor after it fell while being hauled through the vaulting in 1950. The copper disc has beneath it an oil bath in which the weight of the plumb line can hang and remain steady.

Francis Price initiated a scheme for levelling the bases of the four crossing piers and several parts of the surrounding wall benching. Measurements were taken for some years by Price but it was not until 1969 that regular recording was undertaken. Price's levelling points were reinstated with square bronze markers set into the stonework, according to Price's drawing of the cathedral on which he recorded his system of levelling.

### The North Transept

The main north transept is of four bays, the southern one being an extension of the nave and choir aisles. All four bays are of equal height with vaulting the same as that in the nave. The eastern aisle is vaulted at the same level as the choir aisle and is divided into three bays. The bays contain chapels that, prior to the eighteenth century, were screened from the rest of the transept. The northern chapel is that of St Thomas, the centre one dedicated to St Edmund and the southern formerly the chapel of St John the Baptist.

The aisle bays are divided by Purbeck piers composed of four shafts with the stone laid on its natural bed and left unpolished. There are no detached polished shafts. These piers are surmounted by arches that have a central order of dog-toothing, which is common to the arches east of the western entrance to the choir. Above the three chapels, the triforium is the same as that of the choir. The southern bay has piers with polished Purbeck shafting as those of the choir, the triforium tracery has differences in detail. All four bays of clerestory are the same as that of the nave. The east wall of the aisle has three two-light windows; a similar window is in the north wall of St Thomas's Chapel.

The north wall of the transept is of three stages, the lower of three lancets with splayed jambs and mullions with shafted fronts with bases and capitals, the moulding of the lancet heads rising from the capitals. The central stage is of three windows with twin lancets surmounted by quatrefoil openings. Internally is an arcade of three arches supported on cluster shaft piers. Between windows and arcade is a walkway. The upper stage is of four lancets with an inner arcade of trefoil headed arches supported on cluster piers and single shafts with collars. There is a walkway between window and arcade.

The west wall is of three stages. The lower windows are of double lancets with shafted jambs; in front of the mullions are

*The north end of the north transept.*

coupled shafts. At triforium the windows are of twin lancets with plate tracery incorporating a quatrefoil opening. Internally is an arcade of double arches with shafted jambs and clustered central shafting. Between windows and arcade is a walkway. The clerestory windows are the same as in the nave.

The southern bays on both east and west sides are blocked at clerestory level and have buttresses at triforium level. At the south end of the west wall are the jambs and head of a filled in doorway. On the exterior the outline of the door can be seen at plinth level. Within the recess of the blocked door is a white marble tablet on which are recorded several names of the Harris family who are buried in the cathedral. There are several Harris floor slabs, most of which have been re-cut (1985–6). One of the problems with floor slabs is the eradication of names caused by the tramp of many feet. It is, therefore, essential that records are kept and, at Salisbury, it was a James Harris in 1825 who recorded all wall and floor slabs.

Against the west wall stand four wooden chests of the thirteenth and fourteenth centuries. At the south end is an iron-bound chest of the late thirteenth century. There are four padlocks and three rim locks; all have different keys so that it could require seven people to be present when the chest was opened. At each end are two links for carrying the chest suspended from poles.

Next is a semi-circular cope chest, possibly thirteenth-century, made to contain the copes which could be laid flat in the chest. The lid requires pulley blocks to lift it.

The next chest is closely bound with iron, the end boards are extended to form legs. The top is in two sections, the joint covered by a strap secured into a lock. One section of lid has to be opened first because inside is a lock that helps secure the other section of the lid. Again several people were needed to open the chest, each having a different key, thus ensuring security. At the north end is a resurfaced thirteenth-century chest.

Note how the piers of the aisle arcade lean towards the north, a result of the pressure from the tower and spire.

In the former chapel of St John are the large organ pipes and a cross that formerly hung over the high altar.

*The grave slab of Thomas Lambert—he died before he was born!*

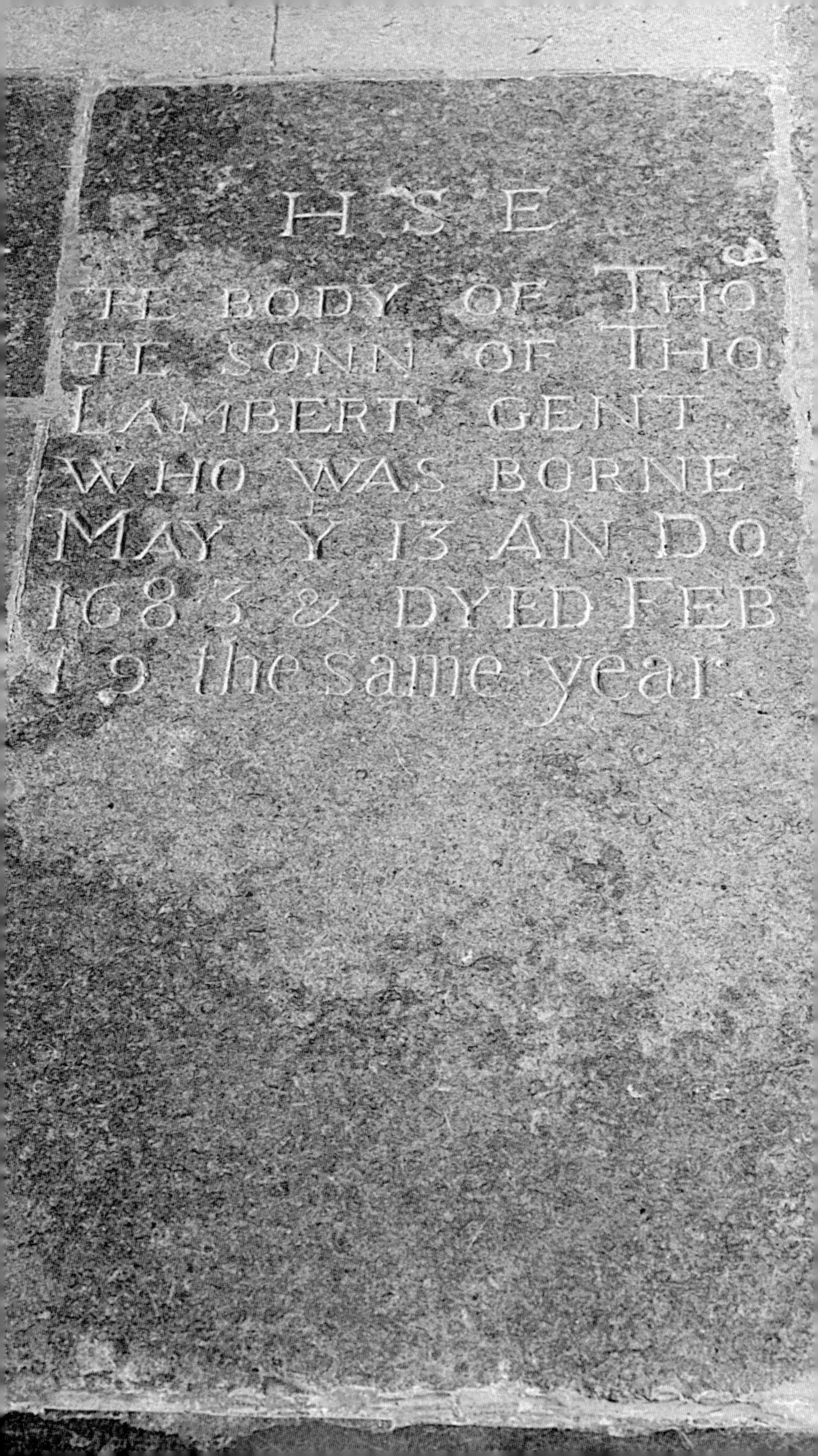

H S E

TE BODY OF Tho

TE SONN OF Tho

LAMBERT GENT

WHO WAS BORNE

MAY Y 13 AN Do

1683 & DYED FEB

19 the same year

## *The North Choir Aisle*

The details of vaulting and windows are the same as in the nave aisles. At the western entrance of the aisle are wrought iron gates and railings by Skidmore, part of a set of iron work that includes the gates and railings at the west end of the south choir aisle, the north and south gates into the choir and the screen behind the high altar.

The three western bays of the aisle form the 'dark corner' of the cathedral, flanked as it is by the northern transepts on one side and the northern organ case on the other.

The eastern four bays are divided between the aisle and that part of the cathedral finished by 1225. The dividing line is at the point where triple Purbeck shafts rise from an enlargement of the wall benching to a cross arch with moulding and dogtoothing. This is the point at which the building would have been screened in 1225, the two easternmost bays forming the chapel of St Peter, and the altar standing where the Gorges tomb was built.

On the pier immediately west of the organ case is a wind speed indicator connected to rotating vanes on top of the spire. Its purpose is to show the speed of the wind when taking structural measurements and to ensure that it is safe for anyone working at high levels on the tower or spire.

On the floor near the tomb of Thomas Bennett is the grave slab of Master Thomas Lambert who was born on 13 May 1683 and died on 19 February the same year.

'Thomas Lambert all should mourn for he died three months before he was born!' The old style calendar accounts for the strange fact.

On either side of the Gorges tomb the floor is composed of thirteenth-century tiles. This type of tile originally covered much of the eastern half of the cathedral. They were possibly made near Salisbury since kilns of the period, and earlier, were at Laverstock, Downton and Clarendon. The process of manufacture and firing was such that not many tiles of the same pattern ended up looking the same. Professor Robert Baker carried out research and experiments before producing new tiles, by the old method, for retiling the north choir aisle at Winchester. He, too, found that few ever finished looking the same.

To the north of the Gorges tomb is a double aumbry that once served St Peter's altar. To the south of the tomb stands a small chamber organ built in 1764 by Snetzler. He was a Swiss organ builder and the history of the instrument is unknown until 1900. It came to the cathedral in 1958 and a new case was made in the cathedral workshops in 1961 to a design by Lord Mottistone.

The door in the north wall in the fourth bay from the east was cut through in 1930 to enable the Dean to have a shorter journey between cathedral and deanery.

East of the crossing the aisle vaulting was originally painted with decorations similar to those in the vestibule of the Chapter House. In the third bay from the west an investigation was carried out to see if the eighteenth-century limewash could be removed. Beneath the limewash the original colours were found as fresh and bright as the day they were first applied. Only a small area was uncovered on the vault, as was part of a boss revealing fragments of gold.

## The North-east Transept

The experiment of removing limewash from the vaults was continued here in the bay of the high vaulting over the north choir aisle. Using ultra-violet light the paintwork could clearly be seen outlined under the limewash. When scaffolding was erected, and the first pieces of limewash removed, the truth dawned; there was no paint. What had shown through was the outline of the oil that had soaked into the plaster. In the eighteenth century the pigment, possibly no more than an unstable powder, was brushed away before limewashing. Roundels can be seen quite clearly on the vault, each one containing the figure of an angel holding a scroll. Under ultra-violet light all the figures can be seen. They correspond with the drawings made by Schnebbelie and formed part of a design covering the choir, presbytery and eastern transepts. In the mouldings of the vault ribs and the arcading at triforium and clerestory can still be seen a great deal of colour. The bosses and corbel heads have fragments of gilding and colour.

This vault, along with all vaulting in the eastern end of the cathedral was covered with limewash in about 1790. The reason that roundels can be seen is a result of nineteenth-century work when Wyatt's wash was removed to the edge of the circular painted panels.

It is difficult to comprehend the thinking that inspired Wyatt to create a 'whited sepulchre' and much was written at the time to justify or denounce the work.

'The vaultings of the choir and eastern transept are greatly

improved by erasing certain paintings in fresco that were thereon, which certainly destroyed the harmony of the roof: Mr Wyatt has judiciously coloured the arches and ribs as nearly as possible to the pillars from whence they spring, contrasting the ceiling and walls with a lighter colouring, which gives every part its due effect. These paintings were confessedly mere daubings, but admired for their antiquity; and many gentlemen were much offended at their being erased, some not scrupling to affirm, that they were co-eval with the building: when this business was in hand, I had the curiosity to carefully examine what they might conceal, and if some probable conjecture might not be formed as to their antiquity, and, on examination, I discovered the evident remains of lines drawn in imitation of brick, which the medallions had concealed; similar lines still remain on the ceiling of the western part of the nave and principal transept. This circumstance indisputably proves that the paintings were added subsequent to these lines: I should imagine therefore, that no one will think such a work to have been of great antiquity: and on no other account could it have been admired.' (William Dodsworth 1792.)

This statement was a defence of Wyatt's work which had roused even the Society of Antiquaries to action. Jacob Schnebblie, an artist engaged by Richard Gough and the Society was sent to Salisbury in 1789 to record the vault paintings, the chapels and some of the monuments. The paintings got into the possession of Gough and thence with his papers and maps etc. to the Bodleian Library at Oxford. The drawings show the layout of the figures on the vault and record what each scroll had written upon it. By this means Gough ensured that at least an accurate record was kept, knowing of Wyatt's intentions.

Dividing the north-east transept from the north aisle is a fifteenth-century wooden screen, much repaired but still retaining its original door and two complete sections of panelling and open work.

The narrow width of the transept seems to add to its height. The eastern aisle contains two chapels, that to the north dedicated to St Martin and the southern (now the Baptistry), to St Katherine. There are distinct differences in the eastern window. The northern one has three lancets of unequal height

*Traces of the thirteenth-century painting beneath the eighteenth-century limewash.*

with mouldings and dogtoothing. The southern window is of two lancets of equal size with plain mouldings. The triforium and clerestory follow the pattern of the rest of the cathedral. On the west side the lower windows are deeply recessed with coved jambs that have arched tops. The window heads are moulded in the form of vaulting. The vaulting of the transept springs from corbel heads and shafting in Purbeck marble, the heads being difficult to see but finely carved.

At the base of the west wall are remains of the original pulpitum, a series of canopied niches with curved rear walls. Between each niche is a detached trefoil Purbeck shaft set against a mullion with foliated carving. In the spandrels of the canopies are angels carrying symbols of the Eucharist and musical instruments. The moulding of the arches is set forward, thus forming the canopies; the hood moulding has carved stops in the form of heads. The carving bears a resemblance to that in the Chapter House.

Although repainted and gilded at some time prior to its removal in the eighteenth century, there is still some original decoration. The pulpitum stood at the western entrance to the choir, had an upper storey, double-arched doorway and, on its east side, the return stalls. It is a fine piece of work and seems to have other similarities with the Chapter House such as the deeply cut foliated capitals to the shafts. On top is a narrow moulding worked on the edge of flat slabs. At least two of these slabs have the remains of relief carving showing. The carving has been cut down to make the slab flat. It is suggested that these slabs once formed part of Bishop Roger's screen at Old Sarum which had a series of carved panels depicting the Life of Christ. Something old added to something new in the thirteenth century.

In the centre of the screen is a doorway that was the entrance to the Beauchamp Chapel through the south wall of the Trinity Chapel. Above an ogee arch are the arms of Bishop Beauchamp. The doorway has been raised to make it in line with the top of the screen.

There is a memorial to the artist Rex Whistler within the recess formed by the doorway. On a Purbeck corbel stands a bronze lantern within which is a prism of glass engraved by Laurence Whistler, brother of Rex. The Purbeck marble for the corbel was taken out of the ground in 1985 from an area that once supplied the cathedral. During excavations to remove the marble a medieval mine was found showing the cramped conditions under which the thirteenth-century quarrymen worked. A shaft had been dug at an angle of 45 degrees through ten feet (3 m) of overburden and some eight feet (2.4 m) of stone. One foot 6 inches (45 cm) of shale had then been removed from under the bottom layer of stone. Into this space were dropped the blocks of marble to be pulled out of the ground by winches. By this method several thousand tons of marble were extracted for Salisbury. The corbel for the memorial was worked by an apprentice following in the steps of thirteenth-century builders.

On the floor of the transept are two memorial brasses, one to Bishop Wyville, one to Bishop Gheast. Both were originally in the floor of the choir and were removed to their present positions in 1684 when the floor of the choir was repaired. The Wyville brass is set in a Purbeck marble ledger of large size. The brass is formed of plates of latten jointed together, with a border of brass and four shields in the angles. The centre depicts a castle and represents Wyville's success in gaining possession of Sherborne Castle from the Earl of Salisbury. Bishop Wyville is shown standing in the gate of the first ward dressed as for the Eucharist holding his pastoral staff in his left hand. Below the bishop, standing in the gate of the outer ward, is the bishop's champion. At the top is the castle's keep showing gateway and portcullis and two grotesque water spouts.

The story told in the brass is of the dispute over the castle and the method resorted to for a settlement. The bishop and the earl agreed to a battle of champions, at which time the bishop sent a letter around the diocese asking for prayers to be offered for his champion's success. On the appointed day each side was called to the combat point and then each was told to go and prepare. Neither the bishop nor the earl would leave before the other until sternly ordered to do so by the judges.

At the next appointed time the judges found several rolls of prayers and charms about the person of the bishop's champion making it, they said, an uneven fight. At the third time of asking the earl failed to turn up and was disqualified. At last the bishop paid the earl two thousand five hundred gold marks and regained possession of the castle. Amongst the lands returned to the bishop was the chase at Bere in Dorset and for this reason rabbits are shown at the base of the brass.

The border inscription is now incomplete but Captain Symons, that intrepid diarist of the Parliamentarian Army,

*The brass memorial of Bishop Wyville. Rabbits can be seen at the bottom of the castle walls.*

recorded it in full on a visit in 1644. The inscription records the forty-six years served by the bishop, his restoration to the Church of certain previous possessions and of his death in 1375 at Sherborne Castle. It is a magnificent brass. As Kite in *The Memorial Brasses of Wiltshire* puts it: 'This interesting and costly memorial may be regarded as one of the finest remaining examples of brass-engraving executed in England.'

The brass of Edmund Gheast shows a full-length figure of the bishop holding a short pastoral staff and a book. The book represents Gheast's work in helping to produce a new prayer book during the first years of the reign of Elizabeth I. The inscription below the figures reads: 'Edmund Geste, Divinity Professor at Cambridge, discharged the responsibility of Bishop of Rochester with credit, and the office of High Almoner to the Queen with liberality, for upwards of twelve years. But after his translation by Her Majesty Queen Elizabeth, he presided over this diocese of Sarum for five years, for the glory of God honourably, for the edification of the Church profitably, for his own reputation admirably. To his own great gain, but to the still greater sorrow of his friends, he exchanged a well-spent life for a happy death, bequeathing a great part of his fortune (which was neither too little nor too great) to his friends and relatives, a still larger share to the poor, and to his servants the greatest part; an immense collection of choice books, almost above the compass of one library, he willed to be preserved in this Church for the use of students for ever. Wherefore, in honour of this venerable and accomplished scholar, and bishop, whose saintly death took place on the last day of February 1578, in the sixty-third year of his age; in order to preserve the memory of so eminent a man, and in testimony of his own regard, this monument was erected by Giles Estcourt, Esq, one of the executors of his will.' It is interesting to read of a man who could so balance his fortune as to be neither too great nor too small!

In the north chapel is a fine double aumbry of Purbeck marble with pointed heads and doors which retain some original portions. On the east wall of this chapel faint outlines can still be traced of a thirteenth-century painted reredos. In the mid-nineteenth century Elizabeth Wickens sketched what could then be seen. She also did a number of water colour sketches of various parts of the cathedral and also paid for the restoration of the circular table in the Chapter House. She was buried outside the Chapter House in the cloister.

The south wall of the southern chapel is the only remaining non-structural chapel wall in the cathedral. There is a piscina and an aumbry in this wall which also has an unglazed 'window' of three lights with ferramenta.

Against the east wall of this chapel is a lavatory, an oblong stone basin with an arcaded base and a carved rim with grotesque heads at the angles. The upper canopy has simulated fan vaulting, an ogee arch with crockets and upper panelling with cresting. An impressive piece of work to wash one's hands in. It was originally in what is now the vestry.

In front of the lavatory stands the font, dating from 1850 in thirteenth-century style. A classical font that stood at the west end of the nave, and shown in prints of the early nineteenth century, is now in Australia.

In the north-west corner of the transept is a doorway, now covered by the remains of the thirteenth-century screen. Access is still possible to the foot of the stairs where the door is still hanging. Unsuspecting apprentices have been sent this way only to open the door and find a wall in front of them!

## The Trinity Chapel

Here, at the east end of the cathedral in 1225, the first altar was dedicated to The Holy Trinity and All Saints before 'a multitude of the common people'. Those who attended from Old Sarum saw building in a style totally different from that of the first cathedral.

Slender Purbeck shafts form aisles in what is, in all but name, a hall church. The ambulatory doubles as an extension of the chapel, there being no formal division. The whole chapel is vaulted at the same level as the choir aisles, the outline of the vaulting being reflected in the three arches immediately behind the high altar.

In the nineteenth century the vault was painted in drab colours with which Sir Gilbert Scott was not pleased, Clayton and Bell having carried out the work while Scott was ill. However, the paintwork does give some idea of the original scheme of decoration, albeit somewhat subdued in tone.

The side vaulting rises from Purbeck shafts standing on the wall benching and is sharply pointed. It rises, along with the main span of vault, from Purbeck columns in the three eastern bays and from groups of shafts in the western bays.

As with all the shafts of Purbeck in the cathedral, they are fixed with the natural bed of the stone running vertically. It is

*Nineteenth-century decoration of the vaulting in the Trinity Chapel.*

usual when building with stone to fix it in the building with the bedding planes horizontal. The great wonder is that none of these in the Trinity Chapel have split, which they would if too much weight was applied to them.

At the base of the cluster piers there are carved small creatures and foliage. Above the vaulting of the Chapel, in the roof-space, is the old glaziers' shop, used during the work of James Wyatt to produce plain glazing.

The details of the side windows are as the nave aisles. The east window is of five lancets, the central one being the biggest. The outer lights match with the 'aisles' of the chapel.

Below the side windows the walls are pierced to form recesses which are surmounted by miniature fan vaulting and a fretted cornice. The small vaulting came from the Beauchamp chapel that once stood to the south of the Trinity Chapel. The fans rise from small heads, most of which have expressions that seem to indicate a bored sense of humour.

Wyatt, in his 'restoration' of the cathedral, created four blocks of five recesses in which the clergy could sit on a step raised above the level of the wall benching. This seating was part of James Wyatt's 'furnishings' for the Trinity Chapel when the high altar was moved from the sanctuary to the east wall of this chapel, putting it in splendid isolation and remote from the choir.

To the north of the chapel stood the chantry of Lord Hungerford. A doorway and an arched recess were cut through the original north wall to give access to the chantry. In building the Hungerford and Beauchamp chantries the exterior buttresses were removed. This weakening of the walls, together with the cutting through of doorways, was one reason given for the removal of the chantries at the end of the eighteenth century.

On the east wall are three consecration crosses. Those to the north and south have been repainted and are cut to receive brass insets. That in the centre can be seen only faintly outlined and was not cut to hold a cross. This is the only one left in its original form, the insets for brass crosses being done at a later date than 1258, when the cathedral was consecrated.

For many years there hung in the Trinity Chapel a silken noose with which Lord Charles Stourton was hung in the market place at Salisbury in 1556 for killing a Mr Hartgill and his son. The noose would appear to have hung in two different places. One was over the doorway in the south wall of the

*LEFT: A fourteenth-century Madonna and Child in carved and painted wood.*
*RIGHT: Modern figures and door into the choir from the south choir aisle.*

chapel that led to the Beauchamp chantry, the other was over the remains of Osmund's shrine.

There is no doubting the noose hanging in the chapel. There is considerable doubt concerning the burial of a convicted murderer on consecrated ground. A possible burial place may have been in the doorway of Beauchamp's chantry, within the thickness of the cathedral wall, neither inside nor out.

On the east side of the piers behind the high altar are gas jets, a row of them protruding from each pier, the last signs of the gas lighting scheme of the nineteenth century.

There is now no indication of where William Longespée once lay or where the rich shrine of Osmund was visited by pilgrims. Blyth, Cheney, Beauchamp, Hungerford, are all elsewhere, removed from this chapel where prayers were first offered in 1225.

### The South Choir Aisle

In detail this aisle is the same as that on the north. The vaulting also bears the same traces of decoration but as yet no investigation of the original paintwork has been undertaken.

To the south of the Hertford tomb (see p. 129) is a piscina

87

that served the chapel of St Stephen, the tomb now occupying the place where the altar stood.

On the east side of the tomb of Bishop Bridport (see p. 133) is a painted stone memorial of Mary Barnston (d.1625) and her husband (d.1645). Above is a framed wooden hatchment, the only one in the cathedral, with the arms of Barnston quartering those of Manning.

It is recorded that: 'On the 15th January 1767, was buried in the south isle of the Cathedral, near the Choir door, the body of Edward Seymour, Esq., of Woodlands, in the County of Dorset. In digging the grave for his interment a sepulchral stone was found, inclosing a perfect skeleton, of the female sex, which was supposed to have been deposited there more than three hundred years ago. The skull was perfectly sound, and lay inclined a small matter on one side: the under jaw was fallen upon the neck, or collar-bone, in the jaw were six teeth, sound and firm in their places; the bones of the legs arms etc were large and firm: and the whole body measured in length six feet and two inches, from the skull to the feet. On the right hand side of this skeleton, and close by the elbow, was placed a small cup or bason, about four inches diameter, and two inches and a half high: and just by the right shoulder, were the remains of two small candlesticks, which appear to be of pewter, or some metal nearly resembling it; these, with the cup, were well nigh mouldered away. What could be the intent of this apparatus, must be left to the imagination of the curious. Lachrymatories and lamps have been frequently found in the sepulchral monuments of the antient Romans; but this seems to be the only instance of anything like them in the sepulchre of a Christian. That the tapers of these candlesticks were lighted and burning at the interment of the corpse, was evident enough; since after a continuance of so many years in the earth, the smoky part on the underside of the cover was very perceptible.' This large fifteenth-century female was found again during installation of underfloor heating in the early 1960s.

Entrance to the choir is through a doorway with a wrought-iron gate, in a wall that was partly rebuilt in the nineteenth century and has a series of niches containing statues. The figures date from the early 1950s.

This is a good point to view the bracing arches. They were built on to the north and south sides of the eastern crossing to bridge the gap between choir and presbytery. The lower arch

*Bracing arches in the openings of the eastern transepts.*

and the upper inverted one join to form a support beam that effectively has support from the sill of clerestory to the springing point of the main choir arcade. The arches have half piers with moulded bases and foliated capitals. At the base of the western pier in this aisle there is a strange piece of half shafting with a capital. It looks as if it were made for something to stand on but its purpose is unknown.

On the Purbeck pier at the angle of the west wall of the south-east transept and the aisle is a merchant's mark. It is dated 1620 and may well be that of someone who helped pay for the work done in the nave connected with the dates of 1620 and 1622 found there.

In the centre bay of the western end of the aisle is the southern organ case with the loft next to it. The present organ was built by Father Willis between 1876 and 1877 and was the gift of Miss Chafyn Grove of Zeal's House. It cost £3,000 to build and was to have been operated by water power. Pipes were laid and a sectional cast iron tank was planned for the inside of the nave roof. Objections, however, about the large quantities of water needed put an end to the scheme. Instead, a gas engine, using town gas, was used. A case of panelled woodwork was built to enclose the lower parts of the organ. But nothing was done to encase the pipes and upper workings. Willis is said to have threatened to remove the workings from inside any case put around the upper parts.

The works and pipes are in three separate areas, north and south sides of the choir and the southern chapel in the north transept. Connecting them, below the level of the floor, is a duct which at one point passes through the burial place of Bishop Woodville. Between the northern transepts is the blowing chamber where wind pressure is generated to work the organ.

The Willis organ replaced one by Samuel Green that had been built in 1792 and placed on top of James Wyatt's choir screen. It was given by George III, at a cost of £1,000 guineas, his contribution, 'as a Berkshire Gentleman', to the work then being undertaken by James Wyatt. On its removal in 1877 the Samuel Green organ was given to St Thomas's Church in Salisbury, where it can still be seen.

### The South-east Transept

Between the south aisle and the south-east transept is a fine carved screen. The panels of carved woodwork are of Indian workmanship and were brought from India and given to the cathedral by Mrs Morris Fletcher in 1932. The screen was part of a refurnishing scheme by Sir Charles Nicholson.

The architectural details are the same as those of the north-east transept. In the eastern aisle were two chapels, to the north that of St Mary Magdalene and to the south that of St Nicholas. The area of the chapels is now occupied by a cope cupboard made from pew panels removed from Blandford Church. At the north end of the aisle there is a double aumbry adjacent to the tomb of Bishop Bridport and at the south end a double piscina; both are of Purbeck marble.

The vaulting shows traces of original paintwork and on the panels are roundels which as yet have not been investigated. In the spandrels of the lower arches, below the level of the triforium sill can be seen faint outlines of decorations.

In the south west corner of the transept is a door that leads to a stairway at the bottom of which there was an external door at one time. It is now blocked and can be seen quite clearly on the exterior. Its original purpose remains a mystery.

Against the west wall, behind the choir boys' cupboards, are two plain benches with backs. These are all that remain of the seating that occupied the nave for much of the seventeenth and eighteenth centuries. Remains of similar benching have been found used as floorboards on the gallery inside the tower.

On the west wall hangs the flag of the United States of America as a memorial to the many thousands of soldiers from that country who came to Salisbury Plain and so on to the battlefields of Europe during World War II.

The window at the south end of the aisle is partly filled in, due to the building of the treasury and muniment room. Below the western light is a doorway furnished with two thirteenth-century wooden doors. This doorway leads into a vestibule built against the south wall of the transept, matching in width that of the aisle.

The vestibule at one time had a fireplace and here no doubt the sacrist had his office. Southwards beyond the vestibule is an octagonal building of two floors. The lower is now the vestry but was the treasury. Its entrance was protected by a pair of doors, only one of which remains, with small lancets covered with heavy ferramenta and provided with stout oak shutters. In one wall cupboards furnished with oak doors provided yet more protection for the treasures of the cathedral. Against the north-east wall once stood the lavatory now in the north-east transept. In the centre of the room is a slender shaft of Purbeck marble which supports the floor of the room above.

From the vestibule a door, still complete with its thirteenth-century locking mechanism, leads to a stairway constructed within the thickness of the wall. At the bottom of the stair, on the sills of its two windows and on the landing at the top are thirteenth-century encaustic tiles. Two doors at the top, which provided security to the muniment room, still have their original locks.

The muniment room is now the choir practice room and there has been a dramatic change from a place of quiet, dust and old chests of documents to one alive with voices. It was here that the Salisbury copy of Magna Carta was kept for many years, lying on a table for all to handle.

The great beauty of the muniment room is its thirteenth-century encaustic tiled floor, one of only two in its original state (the other is in the Chapter House at Westminster Abbey). To protect the surface of the tiles the floor is covered but around the central post of the roof support an area is left open. Here the glazing is as good as when the tiles were first fired, since chests were chained to the post and protected the tiles from any wear.

The tiles are laid on some 6 inches (15 cm) of lime concrete on top of two-inch (5 cm) thick oak boards supported by nine by nine inch (22.5 cm × 22.5 cm) floor joists. Even under present-day building regulations it forms an excellent fire check floor!

Two early pieces of furniture still remain in the muniment room. One is a fourteenth-century press with narrow cup-boards, still with original iron hinges, now full of sheet music instead of Dean and Chapter deeds. The other is a small iron-bound chest fixed to the north-east wall with an iron chain.

These two rooms play an important part in the life of the cathedral, even more so because of the lack of such rooms. Not being a monastic establishment, Salisbury has no 'outbuildings' where various activities can be undertaken. In consequence, the south-east transept, the vestry and the practice room have to double up for more than their usual use.

### The South Transept

In detail this is the same as the north transept, even the leaning of the piers of the aisle arcade. There are three chapels in the aisle. At the north end is that of St Margaret of Scotland with a seventeenth-century Spanish altar frontal. The frontal is of fine needlework and depicts scenes from the life of St Theresa of Avila. She was born of an aristocratic Castilian family and entered a Carmelite convent at the age of 20. In 1555 she experienced a spiritual conversion, associated with visions of St Mary Magdalene and St Augustine.

She had support from Peter of Alcantara in her work. In 1562 she founded a Carmelite house based on strict rules in conditions of poverty and hardship. Several more foundations were to follow before her death in 1582.

St Theresa was canonized in 1622 and in 1970 declared a Doctor of the Church, the first woman saint to be so honoured. The frontal dates from the period following the canonization.

In the centre is the Chapel of St Laurence. The altar top is thirteenth-century and was found used as paving. The frontal and altar fittings are new, the metalwork carried out in the

*The junction of the south transept and south choir aisle. The tomb of Bishop Mitford is to the right. The organ console is in the centre.*

cathedral workshops. The frontal shows a wrought-iron grille with flames symbolic of the saint's martyrdom.

The southern chapel is St Michael's, where Regimental memorial books are kept and where, at present, the Sacrament is reserved.

In the south-west corner of the transept are three doors. In the south wall one leads to a stairway that gives access to all levels and the roof and also to the library. In the west wall one leads to the cloister and another, small one, into the plumbery area.

There are many floor slabs throughout the cathedral and beneath the majority of them are buried those who are named on the stones. The method of burial was in a lead coffin laid within a brick or stone lining with a shallow turned arch to seal the coffin in, the floor slabs resting on the top. There are far too many to give a full description but one in recent years has been viewed by a great many people, in particular children. It is only one foot (30 cm) square and is marked with the initials E.T.!

### The Choir and Presbytery

The main architectural features of the choir and presbytery are the same as the nave but with variations. The main piers, although having the same general plan, have eight detached shafts instead of four. The triforium has differences in the tracery work and the arches of the lower arcade have banding of dogtooth decoration.

The three lower arches at the east end match the outline of the vaulting in the Trinity Chapel, the central arch, the widest of the three, framing the high altar. Above these arches is an open arcade of five arches supported on Purbeck shafts with a walkway behind.

In the rear wall at the north and south ends are blocked-up doorways, the outlines of which can be clearly seen on the exterior. The doors opened into a roof area no longer there. Above this arcade is a three-light window fronted by an arcade behind which is a walkway. At the north and south ends are access doors to stairways that lead up to the roof area.

In 1682 or thereabouts, Celia Fiennes came to Salisbury and wrote: 'the roofe of the Church is very lofty and exactly neate in all things though not so large as some other Cathedrals: the

*The south end of the south transept.*

top of the Quoire is exactly painted and it looks as fresh as if but new done though of 300 years standing'. One hundred years later all were to disappear under limewash.

Daniel Defoe in his *Journey through England* was not impressed at all for in about 1722 he wrote: 'the painting in the choir is mean, and more like the ordinary method of common drawing room, or tavern painting, than that of a church'. Thus two differing views illustrate the opposites in the appreciation of what is old.

Defoe also quotes the rhyme associated with Salisbury:

> As many days as in one year there be,
> So many windows in one church we see;
> As many marble pillars there appear,
> As there are hours throughout the fleeting year:
> As many gates as moons one year do view:
> Strange tale to tell, yet not more strange than true.

The present decoration of the vaulting was carried out by Clayton and Bell for Sir Gilbert Scott. There had been a hope that the limewash could be removed and the original decoration revealed. After an initial inspection and trial Clayton and Bell reported to Scott that they could not satisfactorily remove the limewash without damaging the original paintwork. They suggested repainting and leaving to future techniques the removal of their paint and the limewash. The lime was dampened, to reveal some of the details of the original paintings. Tracings were then taken to be used as outlines for the new work. Although the present paintings conform to the original outline they do differ from the earlier paintings in matters of detail and content. Scott, writing in his 'Recollections', says, 'the arches and walls of the whole choir and presbytery were richly decorated. Messrs Clayton and Bell made a tentative restoration of some parts but not (as I now find) very accurately'. The arch and rib mouldings were painted and the bosses gilded.

The decorations are divided into three areas. At the west end, over the choir, are patriarchs and prophets. On the vault of the eastern crossing is Christ and the apostles; over the presbytery are the labours of the year.

A description of the paintings is as follows:

*The painted choir vault.*

East

| | | | |
|---|---|---|---|
| June | : picking flowers | July | : reaping |
| May | : hawking | August | : threshing |
| April | : sowing seed | September | : gathering fruit |
| March | : digging | October | : brewing |
| February | : drinking wine | November | : felling timber |
| January | : a man warming his hands | December | : killing the Christmas pig. |

St Matthew     St Luke

StPeter & St Andrew   Christ in glory    St James & St John

St John     St Mark

St Thomas & St James     St Bartholomew & St Matthias

St Matthew     St Phillip

St Jude     St Simon

| | | | |
|---|---|---|---|
| Haggai | Jeremiah | Isaiah | Abraham |
| Malachi | Obadiah | Amos | Isaac |
| Moses | Micah | Johan | Jacob |
| Job | Habakkuk | Nahum | David |
| Zacharias | Joel | Hosea | Zephaniah |
| Zechariah | Daniel | Ezekiel | St John the Baptist |

There has been much conjecture about the placing of secular paintings east of the figure of Christ. One explanation would be the original position of the high altar. If this were placed beneath the figure of Christ it would also have been bounded by the only piers in the cathedral with foliage capitals. On the north side of this bay, east of the north doorway into the choir, is a winch of possibly the late thirteenth century. The winch is said to have been used for raising the Lenten Veil from the high altar. For dramatic effect the winch would need to be east of the high altar. The evidence seems to point to a more westerly position for the high altar than that which it presently occupies.

The only parts below clerestory to be painted by Clayton and Bell were the three arches behind the high altar (the paint removed in 1960) and the westernmost bay on the south side. This gives some idea of the type of decoration that originally existed throughout the eastern part of the cathedral.

Salisbury's choir woodwork has not attracted a great deal of interest as most of it appears to be nineteenth-century. Admittedly, there is not the richness of Chester or Winchester, but

*A thirteenth-century carved armrest head from the choir stalls.*

there is still some fine thirteenth-century woodwork, earlier than that in most other cathedral stalls.

The stalls are arranged to the north and south of the three western bays with return stalls backing onto the east side of the central crossing. The seats in the rear stalls are all thirteenth-century, including the misericords. The arms of the seats are carved with a variety of foliage, birds, animals and tonsored heads with gaping mouths. Only one of the misericords has anything other than foliage decoration and this one is of later date, a fifteenth-century replacement.

The front row of seats is basically thirteenth-century but has been repaired, some half of the misericords being renewed in the seventeenth century. The later carving is heavier and less delicate than that of the thirteenth century.

The front desks in the central bay have carved poppy head ends which date from the sixteenth century. The rest of the desk carving, which includes musical angels and some very fine grotesque figures and animals, dates from Scott's restoration.

After the death of Bishop Wordsworth in 1911 it was decided to place canopies designed by Arthur Blomfield over the rear stalls in his memory. Unfortunately, World War I

*LEFT: A twentieth-century angel from the choir stalls.*
*RIGHT: An angelic bench end in the choir stalls.*

interrupted the work and it was not until 1925 that all the canopies were completed. Within the canopies are figures of the Bishops of Salisbury; in 1952 the appropriate coats of arms were fixed onto the new panels together with the names of each prebendal stall. The organ case, by G. E. Street, forms the backing to the stalls in the central bay.

There have been more changes within the choir than anywhere else in the cathedral. In the thirteenth century the stalls occupied their present position but were backed by some form of screen, with the return stalls backing onto the pulpitum. Alterations in the sixteenth century enlarged the number of seats, but the first great change came in the seventeenth century. Defoe wrote in the early eighteenth century: 'The choir resembles a theatre rather than a venerable choir of a church: it is painted white with panels golden, and groups and garlands of roses and other flowers intertwined round the top of the stalls; each stall hath the arms of its holder in gilt letters or blue writ on it; and the episcopal throne with Bishop Ward's arms upon it would make a fine theatrical decoration, being supported by gilt pillars and painted with

*The thirteenth-century choir stalls with canopies by Arthur Blomfield.*

flowers upon white all over.' This scheme of things was that suggested by Christopher Wren.

In the eighteenth century canopies were placed over the stalls, incorporating boxes as in the theatre. Entrance to the boxes was from the aisles. They were lined with red plush and were so dark inside that candles were needed at all times, the candles not being provided by the Dean and Chapter.

A good description of the conditions prevailing is given in a letter dated November 1869: 'The canvas screen is being put up across the nave to divide it from the choir which is to be restored as a memorial to Bishop Hamilton. It is a pleasure to see the screen shutting off the Lady Chapel removed at last. It must be lighter and airier in the nave, where we shall now be for many years. We have had to sit in boxes round the Choir behind the stalls, and to enter them from staircases in the aisles. The box is small and stuffy, the ceiling very low, and the old red baize smells fusty to a degree. There are no lights in the Cathedral, so on winter Sunday afternoons there can be no sermons, and the Dean and the minor canons in course have each a little flickering candle. Everyone else is in pitch darkness, unless private candles are brought. We never expect to see into our books in the afternoon. No evening service can be held in the Cathedral, and the Lent sermons have to be in the parish churches.'

Sir Gilbert Scott's restoration must have been welcomed by those who had endured such conditions. The 'boxes' were cleared away, the woodwork of the stalls cleaned and repaired. Gas lighting was installed allowing sermons on winter afternoons! The Bishop's throne was designed by Scott and executed by Mr Earp of Lambeth. It was a gift of clergy who had been ordained in the cathedral.

Scott's choir pulpit has now gone, replaced in 1950 by the present wooden one designed by Randol Blacking, in memory of Bishop Geoffrey Lunt (1946–8).

The floor was laid with Minton tiles and insets of marble and Scott designed a reredos which was the gift of Earl Beauchamp. All these have now gone, along with Skidmore's screen, the result of work carried out between 1959 and 1962. The reredos and screen disappeared overnight (see p. 29), parts of the reredos have been found (1986) while digging out new drains along the south wall of the cloisters. They were buried, presumably to hide them.

After the removal of most of Scott's work, Lord Mottistone designed the present furniture in the presbytery, including the altar rails.

The floor that replaced the Minton tiles is of Purbeck pond stone laid so that the edge of the bedding plane is shown. Although a fine paving stone, it produces a rather insipid and bland mass where colour and pattern had always been.

To the side of the north door into the choir is a plaque commemorating the distribution of Maundy money by Queen Elizabeth II in 1974. On the opposite side of the choir, to the east of the south door, is a plaque that commemorates several members of the Pembroke family who were buried in the cathedral but had no marked grave.

After the view from the aisle, the Audley Chapel seen from the presbytery has a different aspect. The fine fan vaulting with its original colouring, the canopied niches, the lace-like carving of the cornices over the tomb itself, all this is in contrast to the severe lines of the iron chapel on the opposite side.

The high altar is modern (1984), having been designed by Alan Rome after Scott's altar table was damaged by a fire deliberately started beneath it. The frontal is the work of the

*The presbytery with high altar. In the background, the Trinity Chapel.*

Wessex Guild of Embroiderers. On the altar the cross and candlesticks were carved in the cathedral workshops.

The altar top is of Purbeck stone, similar in some ways to the marble used so profusely throughout the cathedral. The outer supports are of Chilmark stone extracted from a mine near to that from which stone came in the thirteenth century to build the cathedral. In the centre support, three pieces of carved stone that formed part of the cathedral at Old Sarum have been incorporated into the high altar. Combined, therefore, in the most important part of the Church are the place where the present cathedral was conceived and the skill of modern-day craftsmen that ensures its survival.

After 700 years the Cathedral Church of St Mary the Virgin in Salisbury remains a house of God where prayer is daily offered.

*Chapter Five*

---

# STAINED GLASS
# AND MONUMENTS

## THE GLASS

BECAUSE OF THE short period in which Salisbury was built, the original glass would have reflected the style of that part of the thirteenth century. Had it survived, it would have provided one of the finest examples of its period. Many, if not all, the clerestory windows would have been glazed as the single light on the west side of the main south transept. This is of plain glass in geometrical pattern termed grisaille because of its green and grey tints, the colour being a result of impurities in the sand used for making the glass. In the south-east transept there is a larger example of this patterned glazing.

Little stained glass remains, due to changing tastes and deliberate destruction. What may have been in any particular window can only be guessed at. There is, however, within the cathedral a range of glass from the thirteenth to the twentieth centuries.

The stained glass was removed from windows in the north nave aisle during and after the Reformation. Bishop Edmund Gheast had the coloured glass removed and plain installed with his coat of arms in each light. There is little evidence that Salisbury suffered greatly from loss of glass during the Commonwealth period.

James Wyatt proved more destructive than revolution or social change. After his work had finished in 1793 the only coloured glass in the cathedral was the east window of the choir, the 'Moses' window, and the east window of the Trinity Chapel which then showed the scene of the Resurrection, designed by Sir Joshua Reynolds and produced by Edginton of Birmingham. The Moses window is still there, the east window of the Trinity Chapel has changed more than once.

Reynolds was rumoured not to have been very pleased with the result and the glass was removed in 1854. In addition to the two painted windows the side glazing in the Trinity Chapel and the west window of the nave contained painted patterned diamonds. The rest of the windows were of plain glass in diamond panes produced in the glazing shop in the roof space of the Trinity Chapel. The laying-out table is still there and on the roof timbers are the names of some of the glaziers.

An idea of the disregard for the antiquity and value of the old glass can be gained from the following letter sent by James Berry, a Salisbury glazier, to a Mr. Lloyd of Conduit Street, London, in 1788:

'Sir

This day I have sent you a Box full of old stained glass, as you desired me to do, which I hope will suite your purpos, hit is the best what I can get at the present. But I expect to Beate to peceais a great deal very sune, as it is now no use to me, as we do it for the lead. If you want more of the same sorts you may have what thear is, if it will pay you for the taking out, as it is a Deal of Truble to what a Beating it to pecais is; You will send me a line as soon as possable, for we are goain to move our glassing shop to Nother plase and then we hope to save a great deal more of the like sort, which I have.

Your most Omble Servant,

John Berry.'

Like that sent to Mr Lloyd, much of the old glass found its way to various places. For example, at Grateley, near Andover, there is in the church a quatrefoil panel depicting the martyrdom of St Stephen, removed from the south choir aisle.

An effort was made in the early years of the nineteenth century to replace some of the old glass when the west window of the nave was reglazed. From then until the present time additional glazing has been added by such artists as William Morris, Powell, Christopher Webb, Gabriel Loire and by the craftsmen of the cathedral workshop.

Starting at the west end of the nave and working around the cathedral clockwise, the main windows are:

1. West end of nave: assembled between 1819–24 by John Beare, a local glazier, and containing a mixture of glass from the cathedral and elsewhere. Beare in his later years became the clerk of the works and when he died in 1837 he was buried in the nave just east of the north porch.

At the bottom of the three lights are shields removed from the Chapter House and dating from 1265–70. The second from the left is not one of the set but made up. It contains a 'devil' very similar in style to those at Fairford in Gloucestershire. The arms, from the left, are:

Gilbert de Clare, Earl of Gloucester    (1262–95)
Eleanor of Provence, wife of Henry III    (d. 1290)
Louis IX of France, brother-in-law of Eleanor    (1226–70)
Henry III    (1216–72)
Richard, Earl of Cornwall, brother of Henry III    (1225–72)
Roger Bigod, Earl of Norfolk and Earl Marshal    (1225–70)

The larger figures in the lights are French and date from the sixteenth century. They, together with the five heart-shaped medallions at the bottom of the central light, were acquired early in the nineteenth century. The background glass consists of various oddments from the cathedral and new glass from 1924, when some of the old glass was removed and placed elsewhere.

2. At the west end of the two nave aisles are single light windows containing glass that came originally from the Chapter House and dates from 1265–70. At the top of the south window are the arms of Bishop Jewel, dated 1562. The arms of John Aprice, prebendary from 1555 to 1558 are at the top of the northern window. Each light contains a roundel of an angel, formerly in the Chapter House.

3. North nave aisle: Glider Pilots window by Harry Stammers erected in 1950 in memory of the many pilots of the Army Air Corps who died during the 1939–45 war. The depictions are based on Elisha and the defence of the city of Dothan.

4. Next, the Salisbury City War Memorial window by

*An angel from Christopher Webb's window in memory of George Herbert.*

Christopher Webb, erected in 1949. Nurses were not represented in this window, a mistake which has been rectified in a Chapter House window.

5.   The north transept: the striking feature is the north window, consisting of three levels of glazing in the style of the thirteenth century. The glass was produced by A. O. Hemmings in 1895. It does give a good idea of what some of the early glazing in the cathedral would have looked like.

The other windows in the transept are by Ward and Hughes, Clayton and Bell and Hemmings.

6.   Two Clayton and Bell windows are in the north choir aisle between the two northern transepts.

7.   The north-east transept contains in its northern face some fine glass by Powell. At three levels it displays the vision of the Heavenly Jerusalem. The triforium and clerestory lights contain a pattern of coloured glass that includes angels' heads. Very fine, full-size angels are depicted in the east and west clerestory of this transept.

8.   Immediately east of the north-east transept over the dean's door, are two lights containing old glass. This glass formed part of the glazing of the east window of the Trinity Chapel until 1980. The glass is typical of the Salisbury grisaille and is some that was retrieved from the cathedral roof spaces. At the bottom of the left-hand light is a panel of sixteenth-century Flemish glass depicting the Baptism of Christ. The right-hand light has a similar panel showing Abraham with the three angels. The border glass was designed and made in the cathedral workshops.

Next comes a Powell window from a design by the wife of the 5th Earl of Radnor, followed by an Edward Woore window in which the background leadwork suggests the form of Salisbury grisaille with bold scenes of the lives of Ruth and David.

9.   At the east end of the north choir aisle, behind the Gorges tomb, is a memorial window to George Herbert. The design, by Christopher Webb, illustrates one of Herbert's poems, Love-Joy. Herbert was Rector of Bemerton, just outside Salisbury, from 1630–33, and was a regular visitor to the cathedral.

10.   Glazing in the Trinity Chapel has changed more often

than anywhere else in the cathedral. In 1980 the east window changed yet again. In that year the Prisoners of Conscience window was finished. The idea for the window was that of Dean Evans and the glazing was designed by Gabriel Loire and made in his workshop in Chartres. Its colouring is thirteenth-century, its design impressionistic and its contents so varied that the viewer needs more than one visit fully to comprehend the design and its detail.

The side glazing in the Trinity Chapel is by Clayton and Bell.

11.   Behind the Hertford tomb is some more glazing by Christopher Webb. Along the south choir aisle are windows by Clayton and Bell and Powell.

12.   Two windows in the south-east transept contain some of the cathedral's original glass. In the east wall a three-light window has been glazed with glass removed from the Trinity Chapel in 1980. The two outer lights contain thirteenth-century grisaille, the centre light various panels from the fourteenth and fifteenth centuries. From the top they are: two Old Testament figures, unknown; Christ with St Mary and St John; the death of the Virgin; an unknown bishop; St Christopher; and St John administering the Last Sacrament to Our Lady. The coats of arms are early nineteenth-century.

The main feature of the transept is the south window which at all levels is filled with glass found in the glaziers' shop above the Trinity Chapel. It contains several 'patterns' of grisaille and was arranged by Hemmings in 1896.

13.   Between the south-east and south transepts is a window in memory of the Duke of Albany, Queen Victoria's youngest son. The right-hand light depicts Jacob's dream, the left a scene from the Revelation of St John.

Next are two windows by William Morris from designs by Edward Burne-Jones. The intention was to have a series of six windows; only two were carried out. The cartoons for these windows fetched fifty-one guineas when sold in 1898.

14.   In the aisle of the south transept are the 1914–18 War Memorial windows, removed from the north nave aisle in 1924. The great south window contains at clerestory thirteenth-century glass from the Chapter House. The glazing was carried out by James Bell under the direction of G. E. Street. On the west side of the transept at triforium level is a two-light

*LEFT: The twelfth-century grave slab of Bishop Jocelyn. The head is of a later date.*
*RIGHT: The tomb of Robert Lord Hungerford.*

window that still retains its original glazing. This more than any other window indicates what the original triforium and clerestory glazing was like.

15.   The window in the eastern gable of the choir, above the high altar, contains eighteenth-century enamelled glass. The window was given by Jacob, 2nd Earl of Radnor, in 1781. It was produced by James Pearson from a design by Mortimer. Lord Radnor had earlier given money towards the refurbishment of the choir.

Mortimer's design shows Moses holding aloft a brazen serpent. When first installed one critic commented that it was more suited to a ballroom than a church. In some ways it is remarkable. There is no coloured glass, only enamels; there are no horizontal lines to interrupt the 'picture'. To achieve this an iron frame was made to match the main outline of the leadwork. This in turn is fixed to bars set away from the face of the glass so as not to cast shadows. It is one of many such windows produced in a period when traditional stained glass work was at a low ebb. Nonetheless, it forms a prime example of the art of glass painting.

16. In the third bay from the west end of the south nave aisle is a two-light window containing more of the cathedral's original glass. In the left-hand light are the remains of a Jesse window. This glass was included in the west window of the nave in 1819. In 1924 it was removed and put in its present position, thought to be where it was originally. Winston dates this glass as 1240. The right-hand light contains glass originally from the Chapter House, a roundel with a king and a bishop, two figures of bishops and six roundels of angels each bearing an object used in the celebration of the Eucharist. Two other roundels, one at the top of the light showing an angel appearing to Zacharius in the Temple and one at the bottom of the light showing the Adoration of the Magi, are possibly from Old Sarum. There is little doubt that any glass at the first cathedral would eventually have found its way to the second one. Glass was an expensive commodity in the thirteenth century and not cast aside readily; it lay to the eighteenth century to do this. Although the changes have been many, and at times the damage extensive, Salisbury still has a wide range of glass.

# TOMBS & MONUMENTS

The descriptions are set out in areas starting with the nave and working clockwise. Most of the tombs in the arcading of the nave were moved from the east end of the cathedral in the eighteenth century, including those brought down from Old Sarum in 1226.

On the south side of the nave in the arcading starting from the west end:

A plain stone coffin, from Old Sarum and possibly containing the remains of Bishop Herman. Within the coffin are the remains of a man five feet eight inches (170 cm) tall, well built, who suffered from Paget's disease. For many years it was known as Herman's tomb but in recent times has not been marked because of uncertainty.

A grave marker in Tournai marble of a bishop carved in relief whose crosier is piercing a dragon. The border is of foliage and birds. At some time the bishop's head has been changed and the present one is of Purbeck marble. The style indicates the eleventh or twelfth century and is said to be that of Bishop Roger. Recent thinking is that this effigy is Bishop Jocelin. Roger, having died in disfavour, would not immediately have had such an elegant memorial.

Next comes an effigy of a bishop carved in Purbeck marble. There is an inscription along the length of the figure's robe, also around the vertical edge of the slab. It is this inscription that has caused confusion in establishing identity. Richard Gough in the eighteenth century had the slab removed so that he could better see the inscription but had difficulty in interpreting the abbreviated Latin. Daphne Stroud gives a translation in the *Hatcher Review*: 'They weep today in Salisbury for the sword of justice, the father of Salisbury's Church is dead. While he was strong he cherished the unfortunate and did not fear the arrogance of the powerful but was a scourge, the terror of evil-doers. He took his descent from dukes and nobles, and like a jewel reflected glory on the three princes of his house.' Mrs Stroud's argument as to why this refers to Osmund is convincing.

In the next bay is a table tomb that is still in its original position. Exploration has proved that there is a burial in the plinth beneath of a person unknown.

The tomb of Richard Beauchamp follows. At least, it contains his remains which are in an eighteenth-century wooden box, together with the remains of two unknown persons. The tomb itself is not Beauchamp's because the original was lost during the demolition of his chantry. The top of the tomb is of Purbeck marble and has five crosses incised into the surface. It was used as an altar at the north end of the north transept, contained no previous remains and was erected here in 1789 on top of a previous burial. Beneath the tomb can be seen a Purbeck marble ledger indented to receive brasswork. Investigations found a burial but no identification.

Robert Lord Hungerford's effigy is one of the finest in the cathedral. At his feet lies a dog of great character. The effigy was, until the eighteenth century, in an arched opening on the north side of the Trinity Chapel where his chantry had been built in about 1470. When the remains were removed in 1789, they were found in the thickness of the wall, above floor level. William Dodsworth described the remains as being well preserved 'and even a part of the flesh on the upper rib'. Investigations during conservation work in 1974 revealed that

*Detail from the tomb of Robert Lord Hungerford. A dog of great character.*

Dodsworth may well have been right. Inside the present tomb is a long wooden box that contains Hungerford's remains and also pieces of the original coffin. Parts of the body were found to be 'preserved', due to being wrapped in several layers of muslin, or butter cloth, and being buried in a dry situation.

Hungerford died in 1459 and his widow had the chapel built. The interior of the chapel is shown in Gough's *Sepulchral Monuments*. Among the features were the wall paintings, a picture of the Annunciation, a painting of St Christopher and one of Death and a Gallant, which points out the vanity of man and his frailties. Lady Hungerford founded the chantry and provided a house for two priests which is now No. 54 The Close.

The base of the tomb is made from Purbeck marble and Chilmark stone rescued from the demolished chantry. The original burial in this position is beneath a Purbeck ledger incised to receive a brass showing the outline of a figure in armour with the head resting on a tilting helm. On investigation no identity was found nor is there any record of who it may have been.

The next tomb has a plain top with side panels pierced by three holes on each side. The end panels are plain and the interior has a dividing slab in the centre. The whole is of Purbeck marble and is said to be part of the shrine of St Osmund. There is no firm evidence to support this and, if true, is surprising because it means that a large section of a shrine dismantled and robbed remained in one piece. For many years it was known as the tomb of a Lord Stourton, the six holes representing the wells or springs that form the source of the river Stour. As part of the shrine the openings would have been used by those seeking healing. The tomb was at the east end of the cathedral where, on an early eighteenth-century plan, it is named as a Stourton tomb. It was moved into the nave in 1790.

There is another theory that this tomb may have been Osmund's at an earlier date. This is supported by the fact that the effigy remarked on previously would fit exactly onto the top of this tomb. Opinion seems to favour St Osmund but there may always remain some doubt.

Bishop Wyle's tomb is a mixture of second-hand materials forming the base with his effigy on the top. Among the materials in the base are fragments of window sill with stooling from one of the demolished chantries. Wyle's effigy was

*The tomb of William Longespée.*

moved from the north transept aisle in 1790. Beneath the tomb was found a previous burial of the fourteenth century where a hawk had been included in the coffin. The burial is unknown and had been disturbed in the seventeenth century; a token was found amongst the rubble of one Edmund Macks, who ended on the scaffold in 1655 having taken part in a Royalist uprising.

The easternmost tomb on the south side of the nave is that of William Longespée, Earl of Salisbury. He was half-brother to King John and, on his death in 1226, the first person to be buried in the new cathedral. His tomb first stood in the Trinity Chapel and was moved in 1790. The effigy is of stone, the base of wood. An illustration beside the tomb gives a good idea of how it looked originally.

Longespée was a long-suffering supporter of his half-brother, King John, and was active in diplomatic and political missions. He was Sheriff of Wiltshire for much of his life, Warden of the Marches, Constable of Dover Castle and Commander of the English fleet. His activities against the French were numerous, the last being in 1225 in Gascony.

Returning to England, his ship was blown off course and news was brought to King Henry III that his uncle was lost.

Hubert de Burgh, Chancellor of England, asked permission of the King for his nephew Raymond to marry Longespée's widow, the Countess Ela. Ela replied that she considered her husband to be still alive and so it proved.

Longespée complained to the King about such treatment of his wife and threatened to seek revenge against de Burgh. To calm the atmosphere de Burgh invited Longespée to a banquet, Longespée became ill and, on 7 March, 1226, he died. It was assumed that he had been poisoned.

The Countess Ela became Sheriff of Wiltshire after her husband's death and in 1232 founded the Abbey of Lacock. In 1238 she entered the abbey herself, becoming Abbess and remaining so for eighteen years.

On the north side of the nave, within the arcading, starting from the west end, there are: a grave slab from Old Sarum unidentified, followed by two effigies, one of a bishop, the other a figure in armour. Both were removed from the choir in 1680.

The figure of the bishop is small and known as the Boy Bishop. There is no certainty about the origins of this grave cover. There was a medieval custom whereby one of the choristers was elected 'bishop' for the period from the eve of the feast of St Nicholas until Holy Innocents day. Were this figure to be of a boy bishop, it is still not life-size and, even had a chorister died in 'office', there is no reason to believe that the burial would have been in the eastern part of the cathedral. The more likely answer is that this miniature bishop covered the partial remains of one of the thirteenth-century bishops of Salisbury. It was not unusual to remove the heart of a person and to bury body and heart in different places. This may be the reason for this small figure of a bishop.

The figure in armour is William Longespée the younger. He went on the Crusade of 1240 with his cousin, Richard of Cornwall, and fought with Henry III in Gascony with much distinction. In 1249 he again embarked for the Holy Land, this time in charge of the English contingent. He was killed at Mansourah in February 1250. Matthew Paris relates the story of his death in glowing terms. His remains were buried in the church of the Holy Cross at Acre. The effigy is of Purbeck marble and was probably painted when new.

Next is a table tomb of Purbeck marble. From Chapter records concerning the fixing of an iron cramp to repair the top, this is the tomb of William Geoffrey. He was Chancellor

*The supposed effigy of the Boy Bishop, possibly the original cover to the heart burial of a bishop.*

of the cathedral 1554–8, leaving one year before Elizabeth I came to the throne, and managed to live until 1588. Fuller describes him as: 'a cruel man, helping to send martyrs to heaven in chariots of fire'. The skeleton lies in a recess cut into the plinth below the tomb.

Another tomb chest similar to that of Geoffrey is on the east of the porch and contains an unknown burial.

Next comes the effigy of John de Montacute who died in 1389. The tomb chest, of Bath stone, had only three panels having previously been placed against a wall. The north panel is of Purbeck from Bishop Beauchamp's chapel. Montacute fought at Crecy and Poitiers and was steward to the household of Richard II. He was the son of William de Montacute, created Earl of Salisbury and King of Man. There was enmity between John and his elder brother William, to the extent that, when William accidentally killed his own son in a tournament, he sold off all the properties he could rather than that they should fall into John's hands at his death. This sale also included the kingship of Man. The figure is in armour, the head rests on a tilting helm and a lion lies at its feet. The effigy and chest still show colour and traces of gold can be seen in the lion's mane.

There is no burial beneath the tomb nor any remains inside. This then must have been a cenotaph in memory of Montacute and not his burial place. The tomb was moved from the east end of the cathedral in 1790.

The coffin lid, now on the south side of the Trinity Chapel, at one time lay in the next bay. It had been removed from the centre of the Trinity Chapel in 1789 and was moved back in the 1950s.

Next is a double tomb with chest. The Purbeck slabs are indented to receive brasses that show the outline of a man and woman. A pattern of sickles surrounds the figures. These slabs, now reduced in size, once formed part of the floor of an iron chantry erected by Walter Lord Hungerford. The chantry chapel was removed in 1779 and rebuilt on the south side of the choir. The ledgers remained at floor level until 1789 when part or all of a tomb from Robert Hungerford's chantry was used to form a chest. The slabs were reduced in size to fit the new base. The figures in outline on the slabs are those of Walter Lord Hungerford and his wife Elizabeth. Their remains were removed at the same time as the iron chantry.

The last tomb in the nave is that of Sir John Cheney, who died in 1509. A fine alabaster effigy lies on a chest made of pieces saved from the Beauchamp Chapel in which the effigy was originally placed. Cheney was a supporter of Henry Tudor and was present at Bosworth when Richard III was defeated. Richard, in his last attempt to get at Henry, unhorsed Cheney, despite Cheney's 'extraordinary size and gigantic strength' (Dodsworth).

During investigations in 1973, Cheney's remains were found within the tomb chest. From measurements taken, it would seem that Sir John was around 7 feet (210 cm) tall. The effigy, therefore, is life-size. The tomb was erected over a previous burial covered with a Purbeck coffin lid indented for a brass and with relief carving at its base. The grave contained the remains of an early fourteenth-century priest; enclosed with the skeleton were a pewter chalice and paten.

At the west end of the nave are two monuments, one on either side of the west doors. To the south is one in memory of Thomas Lord Wyndham of Finglass in Ireland. He was born in Wiltshire, became Lord Chancellor of Ireland and died in 1745 aged 66. The monument is by Rysbrack and has the figure of Hibernia sitting on an inscribed plinth. To the north is the memorial of Dr D'Aubigny Turberville, an oculist who lived in Salisbury for thirty years and was a friend of Bishop Seth Ward. His fame was such that patients visited him from many parts of Britain, also from France and America. He was visited by Samuel Pepys but could do nothing for his failing eyesight. At the bottom of the monument is this rhyme:

> Alas! Alas! He's gone forever
> And left behind him none so clever
> Beneath this stone extinct he lies
> The only doctor for the eyes

The memorials on the wall of the north aisle include a Boer War one in Art Nouveau style of copper, brass and enamel, the beaten copper work being very good. A marble and alabaster plaque records a train accident near Salisbury on Sunday 1 July 1906. What is surprising is the number of visitors killed, including South African and American.

At the east end of the aisle Henry Hatcher has a memorial. He was a local historian of some repute and is said to have been the author of part of Dodsworth's book about the cathedral.

On the south wall Elihonor Sadler kneels stern-faced at a desk. She and her second husband, Sir Thomas Sadler, lived at Kings House in the Cathedral Close. She died in 1622 aged 80

*Elihonor Sadler on her knees at prayer.*

and was buried 'according to her owne desire under this her pew, wherein with great devotion she had served God daylie almost L years.'

When Elihonor came to the cathedral the sermon was preached in the nave, the congregation moving from the choir to hear it. On the raised plinth of the arcade, holes cut into the stone show where pews were fixed. Here, Elihonor would sit while the preacher stood in the pulpit at the spot where William Longespée's tomb is now. On the western pier, the preacher would see an inscription 'What, not one hour', a reminder not to cut short his sermon.

During conservation work to the tombs on this plinth a pair of small bone dice were found. They had dropped into a joint in the plinth masonry. It is easy to imagine young boys playing dice at the back of the pews, passing the time while the preacher had his eye on the hour glass.

Beyond the Sadler monument is one to Sir Henry Hyde, who was beheaded in 1650, suffering it was said 'the same martyrdom' as Charles I. Hyde had been an envoy for Charles I and was resident in Greece for some years. In the shield at the top of the monument are the arms of Hyde quartered with those of Norbury and Sybells, the latter being a tyger, part lion part wolf, looking in a mirror. So vain was the tyger that by the distraction of a mirror her young could be taken from her.

On the west wall of the north transept are a series of memorials amongst which are: a brass laid in a slab of black marble in memory of John Britton, born in Wiltshire, died 1 January 1857 and buried at Norwood. His series of books about cathedrals and antiquities are amongst the best written in the first half of the nineteenth century. They contain prints which in some ways offer more information than many of today's photographs. Britton, however, did have some disparaging remarks about the spire. 'Although this spire is an object of popular and scientific curiosity, it cannot be properly regarded as beautiful or elegant, either in itself or as a member of the edifice to which it belongs. A maypole or a poplar tree, a pyramid or a plain single column, can never satisfy the eye of an artist, or be viewed with pleasure by the man of taste. Either may be a beautiful accessory, or be pleasing in association with other forms. The tall thin spire is also far from being an elegant object.'

A monument by Bacon to James Harris, author of 'Hermes', shows a representation of moral philosophy mourning over a medallion head of the deceased. James Harris died in 1780 having lived at Malmesbury House in the Close. His son, also James, was created first Earl of Malmesbury and a full-length figure of him, by Chantrey, is shown reclining above an inscription that records his diplomatic career. He died in 1820.

A Flaxman monument to William Benson Earle shows the figure of Benevolence unveiling a representation of the Good Samaritan. Earle, amongst his other charitable works, left 2000 guineas to the Matrons' College in the Close.

At the north end of the north transept is the tomb of Bishop Blyth, who died 1499. The tomb previously stood behind the high altar and was moved to its present position in 1790. Blyth became known as the 'thwart over bishop' because his tomb was orientated north and south. When the body was excavated in 1790 it was found to be placed in the orthodox manner, east and west. The tomb masks the outline of a doorway that, until 1790, was in use. The tomb chest is surmounted by a defaced effigy and a canopy with vaulting. Traces of colour still remain within the canopy. To the right of Blyth is a white marble figure sitting in a chair atop a plinth. This memorial is by R. C. Lucas who, at one time, lived in Salisbury. The figure is that of Sir Richard Colt Hoare (1758–1838), who entered the business of banking but found travel and antiquities more to his liking. Sir Richard lived at Stourhead, a property now in the care of the National Trust. In the library at Stourhead is a model of the memorial.

On the north wall of St Thomas's Chapel is a memorial by Flaxman in memory of Walter Long, the figures representing Justice and Literature. On the east wall, behind curtains, is another Flaxman memorial in memory of William Long, brother of Walter. He was a surgeon at St Bartholomew's Hospital for thirty-three years and at one time Master of the Royal College of Surgeons.

At the entrance to the north choir aisle is a Purbeck marble tomb chest standing under an arched canopy, also of Purbeck marble. Although ascribed to Bishop Woodville there is evidence that it may be that of Dean Kymer. Woodville, who was bishop for only two years, 1482–4, was the brother of Elizabeth, queen of Edward IV and is said to have died of grief after the family's misfortunes. Edward IV was deposed by Richard III and Woodville's other brother-in-law, Henry Duke of Buckingham, was executed in the market place of Salisbury in 1483.

On the opposite side of the north choir aisle is a cadaver ascribed to Archdeacon Sydenham, who died 1524. He was chaplain to Henry VII and Henry VIII and Archdeacon of Sarum from 1503–24. His coat of arms was in the window opposite the cadaver until the glass was removed during Wyatt's restoration.

Next comes the tomb of Thomas Bennett: a cadaver effigy lies on a panelled stone chest in a recess beneath a canopy. Bennett was precentor of the cathedral from 1542 until his death in 1558. On the canopy is inscribed 'Misericordias Domini in eternum cantabo, A.D. 1554.' It would seem that Bennett prepared for his death four years before the event. A shield at the west end of the chest is marked with Anno Domini 155– ; there is space for the final figure but it was never cut. A skull and a mole, both symbols of death, lie at the feet of the effigy. On the east face of the recess is a crucifix on Golgotha, now mutilated. In prints published in 1791 and drawn by Jacob Schnebbelie for the Society of Antiquaries, a painting is shown on the rear wall of the recess. This portrays Bennett as he was in life, kneeling in his doctor's robes and cap. The painting, which has now disappeared, portrayed the power of temporal life, the cadaver the equality of death.

Bishop Mortival's tomb comes next. A Purbeck marble slab lies under an arch canopy surmounted by a finial of delicate stonework. The arch is decorated with crockets in the form of sleeping angels, waiting for the call to wake and assist the bishop. The arch contains an ironwork grille while the grave slab is indented for a brass. The pitch onto which the brass was set can still be seen lining the bottom of the indent.

On the same side of the north choir aisle comes the chantry chapel of Edmund Audley, bishop 1502–24. He was made Bishop of Hereford in 1498, where he built himself a chantry. On moving to Salisbury he did the same. The chapel, of Bath stone, comprises two bays with windows. Above is a carved frieze with shields bearing the arms of Audley and the diocese. Inside, the vaulting is richly carved with bosses containing the arms of Audley, those to the east surrounded by roses and pomegranates symbolizing Henry VIII and Katherine of Aragon. The pomegranate, the symbol of Katherine, was banned after the divorce. These and one carved on the west end of the chantry survive. On the east wall is a mutilated carving of the Assumption. Audley's tomb is on the south side of the chapel,

set into the wall. Some years ago a scheme was prepared for the repainting of the chapel's interior. Fortunately, only cleaning work was done, leaving much of the original colouring still to be seen.

Moving east, the next tomb is that of Bishop Bingham. The effigy lay in the north-east transept during the period between James Wyatt and Sir Gilbert Scott, mounted in a fifteenth-century base belonging to someone else. Scott designed the present base and canopy and recalls in his *Recollections* that the design and restoration of this tomb gave him particular pleasure. Scott refers to it as Bishop Poore's tomb. Poore, however, is more probably buried at Tarrant Crawford in Dorset, where he went after retiring from Durham. Bingham saw the completion of much of the main part of the cathedral and gained the 'founder's' place of honour to the north of the high altar.

During the eighteenth century when the effigy and original tomb were dismantled, a skeleton was found. What happened to it is not known because when the effigy was returned to its original position in the nineteenth century no remains were found.

There had been a great deal of criticism of Wyatt, and his methods, in particular about the way in which he dealt with excavated human remains. Written reference was made to 'the jumbling of our ancestors' bones'. If this was true, then it is easy to understand how a bishop's remains could get lost.

On the north side of the aisle beneath an arched recess is the coffin of Nicholas Longespée. The moulding of the arch and part of the wall above still bear traces of original colouring and decoration. Again there is doubt as to the occupant of this coffin. Bishop Longespée was buried in the floor of the Trinity Chapel. No monument had been erected above it and when the coffin was removed it was found to contain a chalice and paten and the bishop's episcopal ring. The coffin in the recess is thirteenth century but no record remains as to where Longes-pée's coffin was put. Longespée was the youngest son of William Earl of Salisbury. He was 'advanced in years' when made bishop in 1291 and died in 1297.

The east end of the north choir aisle is dominated by a tomb with a double chest on which lie the figures of a man and woman. Surmounting the chest and supported on twisted

*The early sixteenth-century chantry chapel of Bishop Audley.*

*Detail of the Gorges tomb.*

pillars is an elaborate canopy which displays female figures representing the four cardinal virtues; the whole monument is topped by a globe and an astrolabe. This is the tomb of Sir Thomas Gorges, died 1610, and his wife, Helena Marchioness of Northampton, who died 1635. The tomb occupies the site of the chapel of St Peter and here Sir Thomas was buried in 1610; the tomb was built after the death of his wife. During excavation for underfloor heating in the early 1960s a cavity was revealed beneath the tomb containing two adult bodies wrapped in sheet lead and that of a small child who was Thomas, their grandson, who died December 1635. Sir Thomas was at the court of Elizabeth I and held various offices. He married Helena in 1580 and was committed to the Tower for marrying without Queen Elizabeth's consent.

Helena came from Sweden in 1565 with Princess Cecilia, sister of King Eric of Sweden. She became a firm favourite at Elizabeth's court. At the age of sixteen she married William Parr Marquess of Northampton who died five years later in 1571.

In 1574 Sir Thomas bought the Longford estate, some 4 miles (6.4 km) east of Salisbury. A new castle was started but the undertaking proved to be expensive and money began to run out. Sir Thomas was knighted in 1586, made governor of Hurst Castle and given the wreck of a Spanish galleon, thanks to his wife's friendship with Queen Elizabeth. The wreck proved to contain treasure sufficient not only to ensure the building of Longford Castle but to establish the family fortune. When Helena died at the age of 86 years she left behind ninety-eight descendants in children, grandchildren and great-grand-children. The effigies lie side by side, he with a horse at his feet, she with a dog.

In the vaulting of the canopy are carved eight relief panels. At the west end is a description of the other seven, *Septem dona Spiritus Sancti*—the seven gifts of the Holy Spirit. On the east side is Samson slaying the Philistines with the jawbone of an ass. On the south side at the west end the Judgment of Solomon, in the centre, what could be Manoah at the altar. At the eastern end Cain and Abel offer sacrifices. On the north side, the east panel is Jacob and his sons, with Esther in the centre. The western panel is not clear but could be Phurah, the servant of Gideon. The tomb is without doubt fascinating, in advance of the time in which it was built when compared with the Hertford tomb, which was built only seventeen years

*The Hertford tomb: 'like an Indian Pagoda'.*

previously, and different from anything else in the cathedral.

On the northern stylobate of the Trinity Chapel is a white marble figure of Bishop Wordsworth. He died in 1911, having been bishop since 1885. During that time he founded the grammar school in the Close that bears his name. Bishop Wordsworth was the great-great nephew of the poet.

The Hertford tomb at the east end of the south choir aisle has been variously described. Dodsworth writes of it as being: 'A superb monument of various kinds of marble, decorated with numerous trophies and shields of arms, and supporting several effigies finely executed', Britton, as: 'a gorgeous monument of stone and marble painted and gilt'. Canon Fletcher in 1927 thought that it looked from a distance like an Indian pagoda. The tomb is the burial place of Edward Seymour Earl of Hertford (d. 1621) and his wife the Lady Catherine Grey, died 1563, sister of Lady Jane Grey. Also buried are their eldest son Edward, Lord Beauchamp, John 4th Duke of Somerset (d. 1675), Lady Elizabeth Seymour (d. 1722) and her husband Charles Seymour sixth Duke of Somerset (d. 1748).

Edward Seymour was nephew of Queen Jane Seymour and first cousin of Edward VI. His father was Protector and Governor of England under Edward VI and on his execution Edward succeeded to the Dukedom of Somerset. Titles and lands were taken away by Act of Parliament under Queen Mary but restored in some measure two months after the accession of Queen Elizabeth. He was created Baron Beauchamp and Earl of Hertford. He had known his wife since childhood and they came together again in the court of Queen Elizabeth. Some time before the end of 1560 they married without the Queen's consent and by September the following year they were imprisoned in the Tower, where their first son was born. Despite attempts to keep them apart another child was born in February 1562, again in the Tower. Lady Catherine died at Yoxford in Suffolk and on the death of her husband her body was brought to the cathedral. Lord Hertford lived on for sixty-eight years after his wife's death. The tomb was built around 1625, probably by William Second Duke of Somerset, Edward's grandson.

The monument has rich heraldic work: some twenty shields, the most elaborate being the one below the inscription bearing the full Seymour arms, fourteen quarterings impaling Grey sixteen quarterings.

The figure of Lady Catherine is raised above that of her

husband so that both can be seen and because Lady Catherine was of royal blood. The kneeling figure on the right is Edward, the eldest son, that on the left is Thomas, the younger son. The inscription in the central recess reads: 'Sacred to the memory of Edward, Earl of Hertford, Baron Beauchamp, son and heir of the most Illustrious Prince Edward Duke of Somerset, Earl of Hertford, Viscount Beauchamp and Baron Seymour, Knight Companion of the Most Honourable Order of the Garter, Uncle of King Edward VI, and his Governor, Protector of his Kingdoms, Dominions and subjects, Commander-in-Chief of his Armies, Treasurer in general on his behalf, Earl Marshal of England, Governor and Captain of the Islands of Guernsey and Jersey, by Ann his wife, who was descended from an ancient and noble family;

'Also of his most dearly beloved wife, Catherine, daughter of Henry and Frances Grey, Duke and Duchess of Suffolk (which latter was) the daughter and heiress of Charles Brandon, Duke of Suffolk by Mary, sister of Henry VIII and Queen of France, endowed as her grand-daughter and the great-grand-daughter of Henry VII. Equally incomparable by birth and as a wife. Repeatedly they experienced the vicissitudes of fortune. Here at length they rest together in the same harmony with which they lived.'

It continues with a description of their virtues. There can be no surprise from the above as to why Queen Elizabeth kept a watchful eye on them both as she did on anyone with even the slightest pretension to the throne.

The tomb steps upward like a wedding cake with obelisks at each stage, those at the base being carved on all sides with armour and weapons. A phoenix sits on top as a finial, above a shield supported by a bull and a unicorn. The carving of the figures is finely done and the whole structure is rich and splendid even though it may be thought to be out of place in its surroundings.

In complete contrast is the plain coffin lid that lies on the plinth to the north of the Hertford tomb. It is inscribed with the date 1099, the year of Osmund's death. The inscription dates from the seventeenth century, and the slab is now thought to have covered the place of Osmund's burial from the seventeenth century until 1790.

To the south of the Hertford tomb is the altar tomb of William Wilton, died 1523, Chancellor of the cathedral from 1506.

Against the south wall, in the second bay from the east is a monument, in alabaster and Hopton Wood stone, in memory of Bishop Moberly (d. 1885). The monument was designed by Arthur Blomfield and executed by Thomas Nicholls. A figure of the Bishop lies in an arched recess partly cut into the wall. In the back of the recess are four roundels in white alabaster depicting events from the life of Bishop Moberly.

The left-hand medallion shows him as Headmaster of Winchester College. In the top medallion he is preaching before the University of Oxford. To the right he is shown confirming boys of the training ship *Boscawen*. At the bottom the bishop is seen presiding at the opening of the Salisbury Diocesan Synod, which he founded.

In the next bay, on the north side, is the monument of Bishop Hamilton (d. 1869). It was designed by Sir Gilbert Scott and was one of his last works. On each side are five open arches supported on cluster pilars of Purbeck marble with foliated capitals in the style of those in the Chapter House and on the remains of the pulpitum in the north-east transept. The figure, of white marble, was worked by the Hon. the Rev. P. B. Bouverie.

Bordering the south choir aisle and the presbytery is the iron chantry of Walter Lord Hungerford. Formerly, this stood in the second bay of the nave from the east end on the north side. Lord Hungerford had been given a licence in 1429 to enclose a space $22\frac{1}{2}$ feet (6.7 m) in length and 8 feet by 1 inch (2.4 × 2.5 cm) in breadth, wherein an altar could be erected, and a place reserved for his own interment. His first wife, Catherine Peverell, was buried in the chapel. Hungerford died in 1449 and was buried alongside Catherine. The chantry was endowed with houses for the priests and property to provide their income. From this same source the Dean and Chapter received forty shillings a year towards the repair of the spire. The chantry was disbanded in 1545, all its property confiscated and the priests pensioned off. Symonds in the seventeenth century describes the chapel as 'rayld in with yron barrs and faire woodworke on the top'. In 1778 Jacob Second Earl of Radnor obtained permission to move the chapel from the nave to its present position.

The ironwork is original, with some alteration to the entrance gate. The base is of Chilmark stone and dates from 1778. The roof inside is painted with a series of shields joined as with a rope showing the lineage of both Lord Radnor and his

*The fifteenth-century iron chantry of Walter Lord Hungerford, now Lord Radnor's family pew.*

wife from the Hungerfords. The chapel was moved from the nave because it had become 'common property', being used as a pew for the mayor, the bishop when not seated in the choir and anyone, it seems, who cared to use it. After its installation in the presbytery it became the property and the family pew of the Radnor family, a purpose for which it was seemingly unfitted in its original position. The permission for the removal of 'the cage' as it was known, was political, ensuring Lord Radnor's support for other restoration works. The ironwork is excellent and fortunately remains intact despite, as previously mentioned, the door having been altered. Forming cresting around the top of the chapel are painted wooden shields and pinnacles, the arms again tracing the family connection from Hungerford to Radnor.

Bordering the east side of the south east transept is the tomb of Bishop Giles Bridport. Bridport was installed as Dean of Wells in 1253 and Bishop of Salisbury in 1257. He died in December 1262 and was buried 'in the south aisle of the choir in the chapel of St. Mary Magdalen' (Francis Price). During the episcopate of Bridport the cathedral was finished and the first consecration took place in 1258. The covering of the roofs with lead was probably paid for by Bridport. Leland writes that he 'kyverid the new cathedrale chirch with leade'. He reaffirmed the 'Use of Sarum' and insisted that canons should only be absent with good reason and that the vicars appointed in their place should 'hath fitting musical voice and skill in singing'.

Bridport founded the College of de Vaux, which was situated to the south of the present de Vaux Place, just outside the Harnham Gate but still within the Liberty of the Close. The college, founded about 1260, was the first settled organization or government, which makes it the earliest such university college. Students had earlier left Oxford to come and study in Salisbury. The reason was an incident that happened during a visit of the Papal Legate, Cardinal Otho, to Oxford. Students went to pay their respect and were stopped by the servants of Otho. Otho's brother behaved badly to a poor Irish monk, throwing hot, greasy water in his face. The students retaliated and killed Otho's brother with the result that all members of the University were excommunicated and all teaching suspended. With the founding of a second college, St Edmund's, Salisbury might well have become a rival to Oxford and Cambridge but it was not to be.

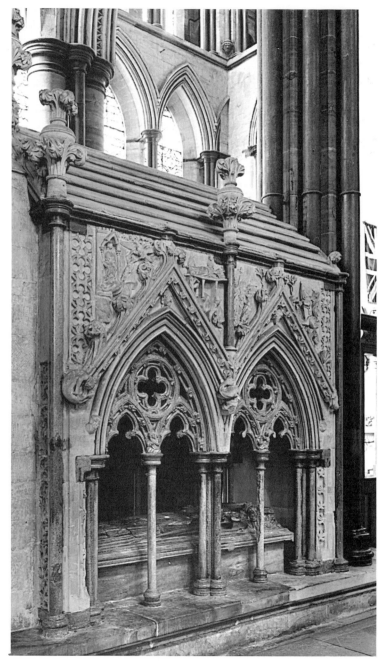

*The tomb of Bishop Giles Bridport.*

Bridport's tomb is of remarkable beauty. It is of polished Purbeck marble and is a canopied tomb with a recumbent figure of the bishop. The figure is in episcopal robes, with staff in left hand and right hand raised in blessing. At the head are censing angels and a canopy. The canopy of the tomb is supported on arcading on the north and south sides, each side consisting of two arches atop shafts with bases and capitals. The arches are subdivided and contain fine tracery work in Purbeck marble. At the west end of the canopy roof is a single crocket of foliage within which is the figure of a monkey. On the edge of the plinth are leaded holes indicating where iron railings were once fitted. Within the spandrels of the arches are relief carvings, four on each side. Canon Fletcher, in 1934, suggested that the scenes, commencing with the easternmost on the south side, are:–

1. Female figure with baby—his birth.
2. Kneeling figure in presence of one other—his taking the tonsure and ordination into one of the minor orders.
3. Seated figure with four others—his interest in teaching.
4. His reception of his first preferment.

On the north side:

5. Figure genuflecting—his homage on being consecrated bishop.
6. An allusion to the consecration of the cathedral.
7. His death, figure lying on bier with angels at head and feet.
8. His body being borne to heaven by angels.

This is the most accurate interpretation of the carvings and covers all stages of Bridport's life. Like so much of the Purbeck marble in the cathedral, this tomb had been turned black by layers of beeswax and turpentine. Having been cleaned, the beauty of the stone is shown to its best advantage. Bridport played an important part in the cathedral's history and his tomb is an historic part of tomb design.

Opposite Bridport is the tomb of Bishop Simon of Ghent, who was Bishop of Salisbury 1297–1315. The grave slab is of Purbeck marble under an ogee arch infilled with an original iron grille. It is similar to the tomb of Mortival but without side openings or cuspings to the arch. The flanking pinnacles have rather nice little heads carved at the corners. The grave slab is indented to take a brass and still contains traces of pitch.

Simon of Ghent was responsible for improving the conditions of the choristers who had been forced by circumstances and neglect into poverty. He set aside rents of certain buildings in the city by a patent dated 6 May 1314 'for the sustenance of fourteen Chorister boys of the Church and of a master to instruct them in Grammar'.

The remains of the tomb chest of Bishop John Salcot, or Capon, stands on the north side of the aisle. It has only three panels on which are shields inscribed J. C. and J. S. Salcot was consecrated Bishop of Bangor in 1534; he supported Henry VIII in his divorce from Katherine of Aragon, became Protestant under Edward VI and Catholic again under Queen Mary. While Bishop of Salisbury he was responsible for sending several Protestants to the stake and for mismanagement of the cathedral estates to his own advantage.

Next, and on the south side of the aisle, the colourful tomb of Sir Richard Mompesson, who died 1627, and Katherine, his wife.. The monument is of painted stone with two figures, Richard, dressed in armour, and Katherine, who is in a black dress with gold flowers.

Originally the monument stood on the opposite side of the choir and was moved in 1877 when the organ was installed. The blank area above the figures was no doubt intended for an inscription. Investigations using infra-red photography confirmed that no inscription was ever cut or painted.

At the west end of the south choir aisle, and bordering the chapel of St Margaret, is the tomb of Bishop Richard Mitford. Mitford was consecrated Bishop of Chichester in 1390 and came to Salisbury in 1396. He was friend and secretary to Richard II. He died in 1407 and in his will left money to keep the spire in good repair.

The tomb chest is of alabaster standing on a Purbeck slab with a moulded Purbeck top. The effigy of the bishop is also of alabaster, the figure having greyhounds at its feet. The figure was originally painted and traces of colour and gold leaf can still be seen. There is a discrepancy between the size of the effigy and the Purbeck slab on which it rests. The slab has a drafted and unpolished area appearing outside the line of the effigy as if intended for a larger figure. Above is a Purbeck canopy with arms in the spandrels on the north and south sides and a cornice of birds with scrolls in their beaks inscribed 'Honor Deo et gloria'. The bishop's remains are in a recess in the

*The tomb and canopy of Bishop Mitford. The body is buried in the plinth on which the tomb stands.*

plinth just below the level of the floor. During the burial of Mary Hurst in 1665 in St Margaret's Chapel, Mitford's grave was broken into and any artefacts were removed.

Against the south wall of the south-east transept is the elaborate tomb of Bishop Thomas Burgess (d. 1837) by the local firm of Osmond.

On the west wall of the transept is a memorial to Bishop Seth Ward. A bust of the bishop surmounts a plaque below which are shown a collection of mathematical instruments and a telescope. Bishop Ward died January 6th, 1689, aged 72 years. He was one of the first members of the Royal Society, a friend of Christopher Wren and known by John Aubrey. Writing on Ward's death Aubrey says: 'The black malice of the Deane of Sarum—he printed sarcasticall Pamphletts against him—was the cause of his disturbed spirit, whereby at length, he quite lost his memorie. For about a moneth before he dyed he tooke very little sustenance, but lived on the Stock, and died a skeleton.' This refers to Bishop Ward's controversy with Dean Thomas Pierce, respecting his jurisdiction in the cathedral and his right to the patronage of the prebends.

On the floor below Bishop Ward's monument is the grave of Canon Isaac Walton, son of the angler, who lived in what is now called the Walton Canonry on the west side of the Close.

In the south transept between the chapels of St Margaret and St Laurence is a table tomb designed by G. E. Street in memory of John Henry Jacob (d. 1862). He was a magistrate and deputy lieutenant of Wiltshire. Jacob was also Major of the First Battalion of Wilts Rifle Volunteers and the tomb was paid for by the officers and men of the Volunteers. It is a most ornamental tomb of various marbles, inlaid mosaics and inlaid brass.

On the south side of St Laurence's chapel is a gothic monument by Osmond to Bishop Fisher (d. 1825), who was buried in St George's Chapel, Windsor. Under an elaborate canopy on top of the tomb chest a carved cushion bears a Bible, a mitre and a crosier. Like much of Osmond's work, well executed.

Against the south wall is a canopied altar tomb in memory of Edward Poore (d. 1780), and his wife, Rachel (d. 1771). Edward Poore claimed a direct descent from Phillip Poore of Amesbury, said to have been the brother of the founder of the cathedral. The inscription claims also that Rachel Poore was descended from the brother of Bishop Robert Bingham, Bishop Poore's immediate successor as Bishop of Salisbury.

In the south-west corner, to the right of the library door, is a simple marble memorial to W. V. Bertie who died, aged just over one year, in 1812. His father had died two years previously, lost at sea. Above the inscription is carved a full blown rose with a sickle shown cutting down a rosebud.

On the west wall are several monuments amongst which is that of Lord Chief Justice Hyde (d. 1665). Sir Robert Hyde came from a Wiltshire family. His mother hid Charles II at Heale House during his flight after the battle of Worcester. Robert's brother, Alexander, was Bishop of Salisbury; another brother, Sir Henry, has his memorial on the south wall of the nave. The bust shows Sir Robert Hyde wearing his cap and collar of S S links. Such collars are to be seen on the effigies of Robert Lord Hungerford and Sir John Cheney.

A white marble tablet is in memory of Dr John Thomas, Bishop of Salisbury, who died in 1766 aged 85. He was married four times and at his fourth marriage the 'posy' on the wedding ring was: 'If I survive, I'll make them five.'

# Chapter Six

# THE CLOISTERS, CHAPTER HOUSE AND LIBRARY

### The Cloisters

SALISBURY WAS NOT a monastic establishment. However, the canons of the cathedral had a similar round of work and prayer as that of a monastic house and the cloisters would have been put to some of the same uses.

Salisbury's cloisters are not as splendid as those of Gloucester, nor do they have the richness of boss carvings as at Norwich, but they have a simple, geometric grace of their own. They are also the largest cloisters in the country.

The walks are each 140 feet (42.6 m) long and 18 feet (5.48 m) wide. The area enclosed is 183 feet square (55.77 m). In each walk there is a rear wall on one side and an open arcade on the other. Each bay is the same, there being only minor variations. The rear wall is arcaded, each arch being formed by the vaulting that springs from shafts resting on the wall benching and having bracket capitals. Within the outer arch are two blind arches of mouldings and shafts above which are foiled roundels. Each bay of the open arcade is divided into four. There are shafted jambs, a cluster of four shafts in the centre and two single intermediate shafts. Above is open tracery work with a large circular foiled opening and two smaller quatrefoil roundels. At the springing line there is still in some bays an iron bar, marking the level to which glazing was originally fixed. All the tracery stonework is grooved to receive leaded lights, and iron glazing frames can be found in some of the squints.

From the bracket capitals of the wall arcade and from the dividing piers of the open side, springs quadripartite vaulting with an infill of stone panels, the undersides of which are plastered. In places in the north walk traces of line painting can be seen, reddish lines which give the impression of masonry joints.

In some of the mouldings of the vault ribs there are still traces of colour, following much the same scheme as on the vault mouldings at the eastern end of the interior of the cathedral.

Above the door at the east end of the north walk was painted a scene with figures and a scroll, little of which is still visible. The vaulting bosses tell no story, like those at Norwich. They are stiff leaf but gradually this stiffness opens out into freer carving in the west walk. It is interesting to note the subtle changes in the carvings between, say, the east walk, the first to be built, and the west walk, the last.

Each walk consists of ten bays of open arcading divided by buttresses on the exterior. After Wren's report that the cloisters needed reinforcing, the buttresses on the east, north and two bays at the north end of the west walk were enlarged. In the face of each enlarged buttress there is a recess, cut to receive the end of a prop which restrained any movement while the buttresses were undercut and extended. In each bay on the exterior are two quatrefoil openings ventilating the roof space. The roof was at one time home for a great many pigeons and a source of pocket-money for a cathedral workman, who went round at night and collected the roosting birds.

In the north-west corner of the cloister is a three-bay extension of the west walk connecting cloister and nave. On the east side is a nineteenth-century doorway giving access to the plumbery. This extension of the west walk was screened off at the point where the modern glazed screen now stands. An entrance from the nave led to what was the Consistory Court. In the centre was a seat raised on two steps where punishment was handed out to those who offended Canon Law.

On the west walk traces of painted shields can be seen. One is a repeat of a shield on the crossing vault and dates from 1480.

The modern screen contains an engraved glass panel by John Hutton depicting St Michael. It was originally in the College

*The cloisters.*

*The enlarged cloister buttresses. The hole for the support strut is above the second weathering.*

of Sarum St Michael and is in memory of a young girl who died in the Avon attempting to rescue a child. Moving down the north walk there is a memorial to Charles Fry who in 1878 formed the first Salvation Army band while he was in Salisbury.

Wooden crosses used as temporary grave markers in the First World War hang on the north wall, remembrance of the loss suffered by some families within the Close.

A cast iron stove, complete with its crown, is a reminder of how the cathedral was heated from 1860 until 1969. There were twelve of these stoves designed by Gurney and Co. placed round the cathedral. Cast-iron flues rose from the stoves up walls, through aisle vaulting, roof spaces and to the open air via the lead covering.

In some cases the flues were taken up stairways, the steps being cut to allow access for the flue pipes. Each stove required three hundredweight (152 kg) of fuel each day during the winter, all of which had to be wheeled in a truck that now stands in the cloister. The dirt and dust from the stoves lay on every moulding through the cathedral and took several years to remove. In the nave the stove that was opposite the north porch was a gathering place where people used to meet and sit. Within 5 feet (1.5 m) of the stove there was warmth but beyond that convection currents carried half the heat to be lost in triforium and the high vaulting.

At the eastern end of the north walk there is in the rear wall a small doorway into the plumbery. This area is so named because of its use in 1260 by the plumbers who came to cast the sheets of lead for the cathedral roofs. The Cathedral Works Department occupied the plumbery from the thirteenth century until 1977 when the shop and refectory were created from the workshops. Around the walls of this area can be seen marks indicating where sheds and buildings were originally placed. The cathedral workshops now lie to the south of the cloisters, where craftsmen practise those crafts that originally helped to put the cathedral together in the thirteenth century.

The largest external entrance to the cloister is in the east walk. This is the door that led to the canons' burial ground. Near the entrance to the Chapter House are buried two of the cathedral's best known lay figures.

Francis Price, who was clerk of the works to the Dean and Chapter from 1744–53, wrote one of the standard works about the structure of the cathedral. It contains a great deal

*Engraved glass by John Hutton.*

*The cedar of Lebanon in the cloister garth, planted in 1837 to commemorate Queen Victoria's accession to the throne.*

previously written by Wren in his report (see p. 19) and there is a splendid set of drawings, including sections through the cathedral, roof plan, section through the bell tower and a plan showing where measurements were taken at the central crossing area.

Price also supervised a great deal of repair work to the main roofs and in 1737 he assisted Thomas Naish and gave advice as to the measuring and plumbing of the spire.

The other person is William Dodsworth, who was head verger during the period of Wyatt's work. Dodsworth's book about the cathedral is a mine of information and also an exoneration of James Wyatt. It has been suggested that Hatcher, a local historian and antiquarian, wrote the section about Old Sarum, that Dodsworth's brother, treasurer of the cathedral, wrote the history of the cathedral and notes about the bishops and that James Wyatt wrote about 'works recently undertaken'. Whatever the truth of the matter, the book is a

145

useful source of information and will always be associated with William Dodsworth.

In the south-east corner of the cloister are two doorways. The one in the east wall is original and opened from the Palace grounds. The one in the south wall, made in 1986, opens into the Stoneyard, site of the cathedral workshops.

Along the south walk is a memorial to Thomas Corfe, who deserves a mention because for fifty-eight years he was organist and choirmaster of the cathedral. He died on his knees at prayer aged ninety in 1863. Thirteen surviving children paid for the memorial.

The remains of the original base and capital from the Chapter House stand in the south-west corner; in the capital can be seen ironwork where the eight rods joined the central column. Here also is the cross from Skidmore's iron screen, rescued at the cost of £40 in 1975.

Along the west walk are various pieces of carved stone and portions of Purbeck marble panelling, including fragments from the Hungerford and Beauchamp chapels. From 1790 to 1860 they were stored in the north-east transept, which became so full that no services could be held in the Morning Chapel.

At the north end of the west walk is another external door, now the main entrance to the cathedral for the greater part of each year.

The four walks surround an area of grass in which stand two cedars of Lebanon, planted to commemorate the accession to the throne of Queen Victoria in 1837.

Within the garth are buried the ashes of bishops, deans and canons. Around the walkways processions still assemble before making their way into the cathedral. Visitors enjoy the atmosphere but, when everyone has gone, there is a tranquillity that was sought after in the thirteenth century and is much appreciated today by those who are fortunate enough to experience it.

## The Chapter House

Entrance to the Chapter House is from the east walk of the cloister through an arched opening with shafted jambs; the iron and glass screen is nineteenth century. There is no evidence to suggest that doors were fitted although an engraving of 1835 shows doors to the double arch leading from the vestibule into the Chapter House. The vestibule is of two bays at the same height as the cloister and with similar vaulting and

*A statue at the entrance to the Chapter House.*

*Purity scourging Lust. Truth pulling out the tongue of Falsehood.*

wall arcading. The western bay has foiled windows and a door which was cut through in 1972. In the eastern bay a door opens on to a stair which leads to the roof. The label moulding has nineteenth-century carved heads as stops.

The vaulting in the vestibule still retains original paintwork. Panels at the intersection of the ribs display foliage and scroll work. Vaulting throughout the cathedral would have been decorated in a similar manner.

During conservation work in 1984 it was found that the original size, used under the paintwork to seal the plaster, could be reconstituted to stick back flakes of loose paint. The bosses exhibit colour and traces of gilding.

Entrance to the Chapter House is through a pair of arches with Purbeck shafted jambs and clustered central support. On the vestibule side of the entrance the moulding of the tympanum is carved with a series of fourteen niches, seven on each side. The niches contain figures representing vices and virtues. The virtues, all female and standing, have the vices at their feet. There have been various interpretations of what each represents and the following list is a compilation of opinion. The list shows the figures in the order in which they are seen:

| North side | South side |
|---|---|
| JOY—SADNESS | JUSTICE—INJUSTICE |
| MERCY—TREACHERY | HOPE—DESPAIR |
| TRUST—INFIDELITY | PATIENCE—ANGER |
| TRUTH—FALSEHOOD | KNOWLEDGE—IGNORANCE |
| PURITY—LUST | CHARITY—POVERTY |
| BOUNTY—AVARICE | TEMPERANCE—DRUNKENNESS |
| HUMILITY—PRIDE | FORTITUDE—WEAKNESS |

Some of the representations are easy to recognize, like Bounty pouring hot coins down the throat of Avarice, or Purity raising a scourge to Lust, who has a serpent between its thighs. Most of the figures were repaired in the restoration of 1856, some were given new heads, but all retain their original form. The foliated plinth in the spandrel of the two arches may well have had a figure grouping showing the Coronation of the Virgin.

To enter the Chapter House is to go into the lightest part of the cathedral not only because of the light allowed in by the eight windows but also because the structure gives the impression of lightness. The slender central column, the tall windows and the delicate wall arcading all add to the illusion.

The wall benching has a lower step which, with the arcading, creates a seating arrangement. On the eastern side the benching has two steps, raising the position where the dignitaries of the cathedral sat.

The arcading is a series of blind arches with Purbeck shafts rising from the benching. The carved capitals are deeply cut in the form of foliage with birds and animals here and there. The recesses of the arcading on the east wall are deeper, the arches forming canopies. In the spandrels of the arcade a series of carvings depict scenes from the Old Testament. Starting from the north side of the entrance and following round clockwise they are:–

### West Bay

1. Description of Chaos.
2. Creation of the Firmament.

### North-west Bay

3. Creation of the earth.
4. Creation of sun and moon.
5. Creation of birds and fishes.
6. Creation of Adam and Eve.
7. The Sabbath.
8. The first marriage.
9. The Temptation.
10. Adam and Eve hiding in the garden.

### North Bay

11. The expulsion from the garden.
12. Adam tilling the ground.
13. Cain's and Abel's offering.
14. Cain murders Abel. Both are dressed as thirteenth-century labourers and Cain is seen with a mattock such as would have been used in digging out the foundations for the cathedral.
15. God sentencing Cain.
16. God commanding Noah to build the Ark. Noah is sitting on the keel of the Ark using an auger to drill a hole such as the thirteenth-century carpenters would have used.
17. The Ark.
18. Noah's vineyard.

*The Chapter House vaulting.*

*The building of the Tower of Babel. A carving that shows thirteenth-century masons at work.*

### North-east Bay

19. The drunkennes of Noah.
20. Building of the Tower of Babel. Here masons can be seen at work while labourers carry blocks of stone up ladders.
21. Angels appearing to Abraham.
22. Abraham entertains the angels.
23. Destruction of Sodom and Gomorrah.
24. The escape of Lot but his wife turned to a pillar of salt.
25. Abraham and Isaac journeying to the Mount.
26. The sacrifice of Isaac. An angel stays Abraham's hand, a ram is shown amongst trees.

### East Bay

27. Isaac blessing Jacob.
28. Blessing of Esau.
29. Rebecca sending Jacob to Padanatum.
30. Meeting of Jacob and Rachel.
31. Rachel introducing Jacob to Laban.
32. Jacob wrestling with the angel and Jacob's dream of a ladder from earth to heaven.
33. The angel touches Jacob's thigh.
34. The meeting of Jacob and Esau.

*Sceen from the Old Testament shown in the thirteenth-century frieze in the Chapter House.*

153

### South-east Bay

35. Joseph's dream.
36. Joseph telling of his dream.
37. Joseph placed in the well. Blood from a kid being put on his coat.
38. Joseph sold into Egypt.
39. Joseph's coat brought to Jacob.
40. Joseph is brought before Potiphar.
41. Joseph is tempted by Potiphar's wife.
42. Joseph accused by Potiphar.

### South Bay

43. Joseph placed in prison.
44. Pharaoh's baker and butler, one rewarded, one being hung.
45. Pharaoh's dream. This is one of the best panels and has not been restored. In the corner of the carving some of the original gesso can still be found.
46. Pharaoh's wise men not able to interpret his dream.
47. Joseph taken from prison and interpreting the dream.
48. Joseph ruling in Egypt.
49. Joseph's brothers journeying into Egypt.
50. The cup is placed in Benjamin's sack.

### South-west Bay

51. The discovery of the cup.
52. Joseph's brothers pleading with him.
53. Jacob and his family journeying into Egypt.
54. The brethren again pleading before Joseph after the death of Jacob.
55. Joseph assuring his brethren of protection.
56. God appears to Moses. The burning bush.
57. The passage across the Red Sea.
58. The destruction of Pharaoh's army. The two-wheeled cart is similar to those used to bring stone from Chilmark for the building of the cathedral.

### North Side

59. Moses striking the rock.
60. Moses receiving the Tablets of the Law.

Originally, the whole of the frieze was painted and gilded. The carvings are of Caen stone and were restored by J. B.

Philip in 1855, at which time they were repainted along the wall of the arcade.

As label stops on the arches of the arcade there are carved heads, no doubt taken from life. They give a good idea of the features of some of the people who were present when the Chapter House was built. The most intriguing head is that representing the Trinity on the east side, a head that is three in one. There are other opinions as to the representation intended, but for such a fine piece of work the Trinity seems the only answer. There is a similar but later head in Llandaff Cathedral.

The windows have shafted jambs and mullions and geometrical tracery. The cusping in the centre octofoil has carved heads similar to those of the arcading; there are very few grotesques, most being portraits.

The six north and south windows contain glass by Ward of London dating from 1860. The glass is a copy taken from fragments of the original and in the tracery are kings and bishops along with small roundels of angels. Some of the original angels can be seen at the west end of the nave. The east window dates from 1982 and was made by the cathedral glazing department. At the bottom of the north light is a panel showing medieval farming scenes and in the centre the arms of the National Farmers Union. The Union gave money for a new window after having held their 75th anniversary meeting at the cathedral.

In the bottom of the southern light is a panel depicting the badges of the Armed Services' nursing units, rectifying their omission from the War Memorial window in the nave.

Supporting the vaulting is a central column with detached shafting. The whole is of Purbeck marble and was completely rebuilt in 1856. Considerable skill was needed to support the whole of the vaulting while the central column was removed and the new one built. The base, capital and shafting are of 1856 but some of the original column sections were retained. The vaulting springs from Purbeck wall shafts and from the central column, and it has fine carved bosses within which lurk strange little creatures and men. The decoration on the vault is copied from traces of the original and from that which can be seen in the vestibule.

The floor is of Minton tiles laid to the original pattern. These tiles look flat and lifeless when compared with the thirteenth-century tiles still to be seen in the choir practice room (formerly the muniment room). The hand-made tiles are full of faults and very rough but this is what gives them their unique character when compared with smooth, bland, machine-made ones.

On the west side, above the entrance, is a collection of various carvings. In particular, two grotesque masks at north and south ends of the arcading in the spandrels of which are foliage and animals.

In the centre of the tympanum is a seated figure of Christ (1856) within a moulded frame at the corners of which are the symbols of Matthew, Mark, Luke and John. The west window contains plain glass, a reminder that the nineteenth-century glass from here and the south-west window was removed in 1962, smashed and thrown on the city rubbish tip!

Wren in his report commented on the Chapter House: 'The chapter house is an octagon with a pillar in the centre; it wants butment and therefore the vault is secured by 8 irons that tie the centre to the walls. They are fastened like curtain rods upon hooks; the hooks are yeoted into the walls with lead.' He then remarks that five out of eight have pulled out and suggests that the rods should be extended through the walls and secured to plates. This was done early in the eighteenth century, and all the ironwork was removed when the column was rebuilt in the nineteenth century. The ironwork was the thirteenth-century method of securing the safety of the Chapter House as the collar to which the bars were fitted could only have been built into the capital of the column before the vaulting was built. (See original capital in cloisters p. 146.) Clutton replaced the bars by a band of iron fitted immediately above the apex of the windows, thus containing the outward thrust of the vaulting.

There stands in the Chapter House a circular table from which legend has it the workmen were paid their wages. The table is ancient but has been restored, its top and bottom frames being constructed in the same manner as cartwheel rims.

Six purpose-made showcases contain various items of plate from churches in the diocese and the cathedral. Much of it was locked away and not seen except on special occasions.

The Salisbury Magna Carta has its own display case. This document was one of a number of examplars or 'originals' that were produced in 1215. All were sealed with the Great Seal, the two eyelets through which the cord of the seal passed now covered from view, the seal having long since disappeared.

There are now only four 'originals' left, one at Lincoln and two in the British Museum, of which one was badly damaged by fire in 1731.

Two people with Salisbury connections were concerned with Magna Carta. One was Elias de Dereham (see p. 12) who, since 1205, had been a royal clerk and in 1215 was a Commissioner for the promulgation of the Charter. Dr Elsie Smith, who was cathedral librarian from 1932 to 1972, suggested that the Charter received at Salisbury may have been written by Elias de Dereham. There is no firm evidence that this was the case but circumstances support the possibility of it being so.

The other Salisbury connection was William Longespée who was present at Runnymede when Magna Carta was sealed. He was half-brother to King John and a person trusted by both the barons and the King.

The Salisbury Magna Carta measures 14 inches by $17\frac{1}{4}$ inches (35 cm × 43 cm) and is written on vellum. The main text, without corrections or insertions, is in 75 lines, the date being on line 76.

The importance of Magna Carta has developed with time. It has become the basis of the Constitutional laws of several countries, including the United States of America. The last clause is possibly the most significant:

'Wherefore it is our will and command that the English church shall be free and that men in our kingdom shall have and keep all these liberties, rights, and concessions, freely and quietly, fully and wholly, for themselves and their heirs, of us and our heirs, for ever.'

This document was first taken to Old Sarum, then brought down to the new cathedral, has twice been mislaid, and even kept for safe-keeping under a librarian's bed. Despite this, it is the best of the four remaining copies and still clearly proclaims its message.

## The Library

Above the five northern bays of the east walk of the cloisters is the cathedral library. The building has a low pitched lead roof behind parapets with trefoil headed arcading. The walls are divided by pilaster buttresses between which are square-headed windows. One window on the east side was filled in when a fireplace was constructed. During the nineteenth century the window at the south end replaced a smaller one of the fifteenth. At one time the mid-fifteenth-century building filled

157

*Interior of the library, showing bookcases made from the timber grown in the Close.*

the whole length of the upper part of the east cloister walk.

The room is entered at its north-east corner where there is access to the stairway in the south-west angle of the south transept. Between the stairway and library is a landing with vaulting and carved bosses. The door is original and still has original ironwork. The hood moulding of the inner face of the door arch has carved stops, representing, it is said, the heads of Henry VI and Bishop Aiscough.

The library's history began at Old Sarum, where Bishop Osmund formed the nucleus of Salisbury's collection and, according to William of Malmesbury, transcribed and bound many of the manuscripts himself.

There are in the library some 190 manuscripts dating from the ninth to the fifteenth century, amongst which are over fifty written between 1089 and 1125 and produced at Old Sarum. They are not illuminated to the extent of other manuscripts, but were produced economically for their content rather than their decoration.

Two of the medieval manuscripts that are especially precious are tenth-century psalters. One is the Gallican Psalter, finely written and illuminated with initial letters wherein sport birds and dragons. The other psalter contains the Latin psalms of Jerome's 'Gallican' and 'Hebrew' versions, written in parallel columns.

Gifts of books have been made to the library on many occasions by various bishops and canons. Amongst the four-teenth- and fifteenth-century benefactors were Henry de la Wyle and Ralph of York, both chancellors of the cathedral, and Thomas Cyrcetur, canon (died c. 1452).

Bishop John Jewel (1560–71) refurnished the library and provided new bookcases. Due to a misunderstanding, many earlier references to the library give the building date as sixteenth century.

Bishop Edmund Gheast (1571–7) bequeathed to the library a large collection of books by the sixteenth-century Protestant reformers, some 1,000 of these books remaining at Salisbury and forming one of the largest such collections in the country. He had many specially bound and many contain annotations in his own hand. This gift marked the beginning of the library's collection of printed books.

Bishop Seth Ward (1667–88) bequeathed 300 books on subjects including medicine, mathematics and astronomy by such authors as Copernicus, Galileo, Kepler and William Harvey (including a first edition of Harvey's work on blood circulation). Many of Bishop Ward's books are presentation copies inscribed by authors such as Nicolaus Mercator, Edward Pocock, Ulugh Beigh, John Collins and Dean Thomas Pierce.

Canon Isaac Walton not only gave books but also money to enable someone to be in attendance at the library. Amongst the books were thirty that had belonged to his father, the famous angler.

Further donations of books came in the nineteenth century from Dean Hamilton and, early this century, from Bishop Wordsworth.

When the move from Old Sarum was made, the muniments and manuscripts (including Salisbury's copy of Magna Carta of 1215) may well have been placed in the Parvis Room over the north porch. The building of the treasury and muniment room against the south end of the south-east transept resulted in the manuscripts and archives being housed in a more convenient and secure place.

In 1445 certain of the canons felt it would be desirable to build a room that could be part library and part lecture room, the cost of this to be met by Bishop Aiscough and the Dean and Chapter. The following year the Abbess of Shaftesbury was given a cope for granting the Dean and Chapter stone from the Abbey's quarry at Tisbury in order to build the new library. The cathedral at last had somewhere to keep its books and manuscripts.

The building remained in its original form until the eighteenth century when the southern half was demolished and a new and lower roof put on the northern part.

A visitor to Salisbury in the early eighteenth century described the library: '. . . about one third of the length is taken up by a place where the Cancellarius Ecclesie used to read Divinity Lectures, at which all the clergy within the City of Sarum were . . . required to be present, but these have for many years been omitted and the chancellor preaches on all holidays in lieu of them. The room is fitted up with a Pulpit and seats proper to the use. The library is fitted up with seats and cases for books in a very ancient but ordinary manner. They are not numerous but some very useful and valuable among them. There are above 100 Mss. chiefly of the Fathers and School Divines.'

Indifference towards the library during the eighteenth century is reflected by the relatively few printed books of that period in the collection. It was also the period during which the library was reduced in size to relieve weight from the east cloister walk. Although this demolition was carried out with the best of intentions, the result has been restricted space in the library today.

Sir Thomas Phillipps in the 1820s paid for some manuscripts to be rebound. He described them as being 'in a shameful state'. Later, he wrote: 'the jackdaws, with free ingress and egress, nightly found both perch and dormitory on the piles of choice volumes, including an Anglo-Saxon MS, which were heaped up in a state of chaos on the tables within'.

With some of the gifts of books had come an odd assortment of cases in which they had been kept. When in 1978 urgent repairs were needed in the library, the Dean and Chapter commissioned a new set of furniture, bookcases, manuscript cupboards and the like. From designs by Alan Rome, the furniture was made in the cathedral workshops from timber that had grown in the Close. In 1983 the work was finished and the library re-opened for study only. Application to use the library should be made in writing to the librarian. The business documents which form the Chapter muniments are now kept in special strongrooms. The interior is now worthy of the fine and valuable collection of books and manuscripts that was started at Old Sarum and continues today.

*Chapter Seven*

# THE CATHEDRAL CLOSE, ITS BUILDINGS, WALL AND GATEWAYS

THERE IS NO doubting that the surroundings of the cathedral enhance its architecture. In turn, it is the cathedral that gives the Close its unique flavour. Houses have grown up around the cathedral, many still occupying sites allocated to canons in the thirteenth century. To the north, west and east of the cathedral are lawns surrounded by a low wall which marks the area of the churchyard. The Close is bounded to the north and east by a wall which continues along part only of the southern boundary. The west and south are bounded by rivers. The area contained within this boundary is approximately a third of a square mile (86 hectares).

Water courses and ditches ran through the Close, and the north and east boundaries were marked by ditches until the building of the wall in the fourteenth century. The earliest buildings in the Close were the masons' lodges and a wooden chapel. The site of the chapel is unknown but the position of the lodges is more easily established. During the installation of exterior floodlighting in 1973 pits had to be dug in the churchyard to contain the light fittings. In the pits to west and north-west was found banker rubble—the chippings and dust which accumulate during the working of stone. In an arc from the west front to the north porch there is a layer of rubble some 2 feet 6 inches (75 cm) deep, a quantity of rubble which could only have originated from the thirteenth century.

Contemporary with the cathedral was the building of the detached bell tower. In the summer the grass on top of the buried foundations dies back revealing in outline the largest detached bell tower built in England. It had a square ground plan with three buttresses on each face and an entrance at the east end of the south face. The lower storey was vaulted with a single Purbeck pier in the centre of the room. This pier continued through the upper room to act as a support for the bell frame. In the south-east corner of the building a stairway gave access to the first floor, which was the ringing chamber, and then into the wooden upper storeys. The three upper storeys were of wooden framing covered with lead and consisted of a square bell chamber, an octagonal lantern and a spire surmounted by a cross and vane. It must have formed an impressive structure standing 200 feet (60.96 m) tall, just 20 feet (6.096 m) short of the cathedral tower.

There is little doubt that the bell tower was built at the same time as the cathedral. The mouldings of the buttresses were exactly the same as those on the buttresses of the cathedral. Its building date was 1240–60, at the same period as the finishing of the nave and the completion of the cloisters. At this time also it must have been fitted with bells. It was never intended that bells should hang in the central tower of the cathedral.

The number of original bells is unknown, but by 1319 there were complaints about the ringing of bells. Rules as to their use and the length of time they were to be rung were laid down, amongst which was one that stated. . . . 'ringing of bells shall continue until the most distantly placed canon could with ease get to the Cathedral', an instruction that must have taxed the imagination of the ringers! There was also a lack of supervision of the altarists who rang the bells. These were normally choristers whose voices had broken. In 1331 the Treasurer was taken to task by the Dean and Chapter because 'the bells in the belfry, with much art suspended, of great weight and price, and sweet sounding to the ears, by fault of officers are suffered to decay, and rendered totally useless for ringing'. A new bell was provided in 1480 and may well have been connected with the canonization of Osmund a little while before. There is mention of a tenth bell in 1531 but by 1635 the number had been reduced to eight.

In 1645 the tower was occupied by a Parliamentarian force under Colonel Ludlow as a guard room and observation post. After a skirmish near Amesbury with Royalists, Ludlow

*1740 print of the cathedral showing the detached bell tower.*

withdrew to Salisbury, placing prisoners taken in the bell tower. A Royalist commander was also imprisoned, as a result of which the bell tower was attacked. The Parliamentarians did not capitulate until the Royalists compelled a charcoal burner to place a load of charcoal, which he was bringing to Salisbury, against the tower door and set fire to it, compelling the garrison to surrender.

The official report refers to five officers, eighty men and one hundred and fifty horses captured and reads as if they were all in a room 36 feet (33.4 metres) square! In truth, some were billeted in the cloister.

An assortment of shops and houses had been built over the years around the bell tower, one of which by the seventeenth century had become an ale house. In 1627 the Court of Quarter Sessions suppressed all ale houses in the Close, except that kept by Hugh Maunds, a ringer and employee of the Dean and Chapter.

By an Act of the Chapter dated 12 March, 1757, it was ordered that 'no liquor of any kind whatsoever shall be sold at the belfry'. The ground floor room had become an ale house and residents of the Close complained about the rowdy behaviour of the drinkers.

The bells, were frequently neglected and although the number six was recast in 1661, others in the tower needed rehanging. During the Whitsun Fair it was the practice of some to bribe the sexton to allow them to 'jumble the bells'. This did little good and could account for some of the cracked ones.

Bishop John Hume in 1777 gave permission for the useless bells to be sold and Mr Lush the clerk of the works was instructed to 'sell the bells that are down in the belfry for the benefit of the fabric'.

An advertisement in the Salisbury and Winchester Journal on 15 March, 1790, spelt the end of the finest structure of its kind in England: 'Salisbury. To builders or persons engaged in building. To be sold, in any quantity and upon reasonable terms, the materials of a very large building: Consisting mainly of stone, ashlar, Rubble walling, Oak Timber, Lead, Iron, Slates, Tiling, and various Articles of inside finishing, the particulars of which may be known by applying to Mr. Matthews Clerk of the Works carrying on at the Cathedral at this time.' Thus was advertised the bell tower. The reasoning behind the sale was one of money; it was cheaper to demolish than repair.

Dodsworth writes that the tower had not been in use since 1745, 'and as it greatly intercepted the most striking view of the structure, it was taken down, and the produce of the materials employed in making the repairs. Thus on entering the cemetery, the eye is enabled to catch at one view the whole of the building, which appears on this side with peculiar grandeur and effect.' This sounds like Wyatt's obsession with vistas and views, and he may well have been consulted.

Mr Henry Ford of Wilton made a successful bid of £500 for the bell tower and a tenement that joined it. The money was used for the redemption of the lease on a building nearby and to help with the work on the cathedral being undertaken by James Wyatt. All that now remains are a few brown marks on the grass during summer months.

The churchyard was a burial place from the thirteenth century until the eighteenth century. John Byng's remarks (see p. 21) give an idea of the state of the churchyard in 1782, open ditches taking away surface water as well as some of the waste and sewage from houses in the Close. During summer months the smell from the stagnating water must have been fairly strong. The demolition of the bell tower was followed by the levelling of the churchyard and the building of culverts to replace the drainage channels. Excavations have shown the use of second-hand materials for forming the culverts. On the east side of the churchyard a small culvert is built of materials salvaged from the Beauchamp and Hungerford chapels. During the levelling work grave stones on which the names could not be read were used for repairing the eastern floor in the cathedral; where the names could be read, the stones were laid flat and buried.

From 1790 until about 1820 many trees were planted, including a number of Cornish elms planted in 1815 to commemorate the Battle of Waterloo. In 1975 they had to be cut down because of elm bark disease. The timber has been used for various items of furniture including new bookcases in the library so that the trees have lived on in the shape of furniture. To replace the loss a replanting programme has been undertaken to provide specimen trees of different varieties.

The wall that forms something like half of the boundary of the Close still contains some original sections. The best of these is the southern end of the east wall. Here, in the grounds of the former Bishop's Palace, the walkway is still intact and of original width with steps to gain access.

The wall was built in the fourteenth century to keep out intruders and those who occasionally came to pilfer and steal. It would also ensure the privacy of the Close, which it still, at times, enjoys today.

The wall was started by 1333 but ten years later work was still going on and its completion date is not known. The stone for building the wall came partly from Old Sarum. The eastern wall in particular contains many fragments of Norman carving. Also of interest are the numerous masons' marks that can be found, signatures of some of the masons who built the first cathedral.

There are now four gateways giving access to the Close, all of them coeval with the building of the wall. At the southern end is the Harnham gate, the only one without an upper room. It has a simple arched opening, a pair of oak gates dating from the 1960s and a frieze of decoration, including a grotesque head. This gate leads through to de Vaux Place, where once stood the college of that name, and to the bridge built during the time of Bishop Bingham.

Giving direct access to the grounds of the former Bishop's Palace is the Queen's Gate. This is the southern of the two eastern entrances and was known as the Bishop's Gate until 1974, when Queen Elizabeth II came to distribute Maundy money. She came through this entrance on her way to the cathedral, at which time the name was changed. The archway has a room above it and is flanked by later buildings.

St Ann's gate in the eastern wall leads from the Close to St Ann's Street, formerly the main route out of Salisbury towards Southampton. The arch has a room above, which was originally a chapel, the window on the east side having two lights with tracery. On this side also are two corbels whose origins were at Old Sarum. Adjoining the gateway to the south is a projecting bay window, the small room behind having access to the walkway of the wall. From the window there is a view along half the eastern wall and the room was possibly used by a nightwatchman. The chapel was for many years leased with Malmesbury House. It was used by James Harris in the eighteenth century for private concerts and theatrical performances. During World War II a U.S. army lorry came down St Ann's Street and tried to enter the Close. The result was one lorry stuck beneath the inner arch covered in fallen masonry. The oak doors date from 1975, after the original ones were demolished by a runaway horse!

The North Gate, now known as the High Street Gate, is the only entrance for vehicles. Giving access to the centre of the city this was and still is the most used entrance. The gateway has a flat pointed arch with mouldings. On the north side there are carved spandrels and above the arch a course of quatrefoil panels. There are two two-light windows with the Stuart Royal coat of arms between. There is a parapet with blind arcading and crenellations. On the south side a niche between a pair of windows contains a figure of Edward VII. On this side fragments of Norman carvings can be seen.

The archway has oak gates made by the Cathedral Works Department in 1981 after a car had been deliberately driven through the previous set. Inside the northern arch is a portcullis groove, the winch, presumably, having been in the room above. For many years, until 1969, this room was used by the cathedral clerk of the works. To the east of the gate lived the gatekeeper and a small room now used only by the nightwatchman was once the Close gaol.

The Close Gates are still locked at night with a nightwatch-

*The Bishop's Palace, now the cathedral school.*

man on duty at the High Street gate to allow residents access. On the west side of the road leading from the gate are the houses in which the Close Constable and his assistant live, the Constable being responsible for the security of the Close.

The houses that occupy the perimeter of the Close form a miniature townscape of their own. Roads bordering the churchyard to the north and west are named as walks. To the east is the Bishops Walk, leading to the gates of the former Palace. Running south from the churchyard is the Broad Walk, a wide gravelled pathway bordering the road at the end of which three houses are grouped as if at the end of a country lane. Off the North Walk leads Rosemary Lane. Similar lanes once led to the city chequers. Around Choristers Green is perhaps one of the finest groupings of buildings to be seen in any provincial town.

The more notable houses in the Close are listed below:

### The Palace
This was the Bishop's Palace until 1946 and now houses the Cathedral School. The palace was started at the same time as

167

the cathedral and when first finished probably consisted of little more than a hall with an undercroft. The latter still remains, serving as a dining hall for the school.

Bishop Beauchamp (1450–82) carried out enlargements, building a big hall and the tower that bears his name. Parliament in the seventeenth century sold the palace, according to one account, to two brothers by name of Barter, who pulled down part of the hall and turned the rest of the building into an inn. Bishop Seth Ward restored the damage and in the eighteenth century Shute Barrington added a porch and windows in the west wing, designed by Sir Robert Taylor with 'liberal but tasteless innovation'.

Some idea of the palace in the sixteenth century is gained from a letter written by Herman Folkerzheimer in 1563 about his visit to Salisbury and his meeting with Bishop Jewel: 'His palace, in the first place, is so spacious and magnificent that even sovereigns may, and are wont to be suitably entertained there, whenever they come to these parts. Next, there is a most extensive garden, kept up with especial care, so that in the levelling, laying out, and variety, nothing seems to have been overlooked. A most limpid stream runs through the midst of it, which, though agreeable in itself, is rendered much more pleasant and delightful by the swans swimming upon it, and the abundance of fish, which (the bishop) is now causing to be enclosed in an iron lattice-work.'

The lake which was once fed from the river on the west side of the Close now only contains ground water and is much reduced in size. It was from this south side of the cathedral that Constable painted his well-known 'View from the Bishop's Garden'. John Constable (d. 1837) was a friend of John Fisher, Archdeacon of Berkshire, then in the diocese, and stayed with him on many occasions at the house known as Leadenhall.

Starting in the south-west corner of the Close and moving northwards, the following houses are worth attention:

### No. 70, Leadenhall—'Aula Plumbea'

Here Elias de Dereham built himself a house which gained its name no doubt from the roof covering of lead. It is possible that this house served as a pattern for other canons' residences. The building cost, however, was so high that Elias had to leave his successors to pay off the cost. In the fifteenth century Henry Chicheley lived here. He became Archbishop of Canterbury and a supporter of Henry V's campaign in France. In 1718

*Leadenhall—built on the foundations of the thirteenth-century house of Elias de Dereham.*

most of the original building was removed and the present house built. Part of Elias's house remained standing until pulled down in 1910 when fragments of window masonry were incorporated in a garden wall.

### No. 69, Walton Canonry

This house was rebuilt in 1719 by Francis Eyre on the site of a house destroyed by fire at the end of the seventeenth century. At one time Canon Isaac Walton, son of the famous angler lived here. Canon Walton bequeathed many of his books to

*The King's House now the Salisbury Museum.*

the library. The house, like so many in the Close, is raised above a half basement. This not only prevented damage to the raised ground floor from flooding but created a basement in an area with a high ground water level.

### No. 68, Myles Place

Sir Arthur Bryant lived here for several years until his death in 1985. Built by William Swanton in the early eighteenth century it presents a rather severe face to the world. Here again steps lead up to a raised ground floor. Like all the houses on this side of the Close the garden runs down to the river. Dr. Heale, the first physician at the Salisbury Infirmary, lived here in the eighteenth century.

### King's House—Old Deanery

This complex assortment of buildings now houses the Salisbury Museum, one of the best provincial museums in England.

First called Sherborne House, it was the prebendal mansion of the Abbots of Sherborne up to the Reformation. After the Reformation several smaller properties were absorbed into Sherborne House. This joining together of houses has created possibly the best grouping of architectural features in the Close, an ad hoc mixture of great charm.

This was the site of one of the original houses and around it were built a series of chantry houses while, to the north, was the deanery. The porch is late fourteenth-century with fan vaulting. There are remains of the fourteenth-century roof of the former hall and much sixteenth- and seventeenth-century work. The property has been sub-divided and then put into one on several occasions. Thomas Sadler lived here in the seventeenth century and it is from his period that the property became known as King's House, perhaps because of royal visitors. In the eighteenth century it was sub-divided into four houses, one being a girls' school. In 1785 Lieut. General Henry Shrapnell lived here, his name forever associated with the shell he invented. Godolphin School occupied a part of King's House between 1837 and 1847 and, between 1841 and 1980, a teacher-training college occupied another part.

The college expanded and new buildings gradually spread northwards encompassing the Old Deanery. This building, like King's House, had grown from a simple hall into a complex mixture of additions and enlargements. In 1948 an inspection of the property failed to reveal any substantial part of the thirteenth-century work. The college was in the midst of expansion and wanted to remove the old buildings to make way for new accommodation. In 1959, after part of the Old Deanery had been demolished and a new brick building placed between it and the Close, the Royal Commission on Historical Monuments carried out a survey and found the original hall which, over the centuries, had been infilled with a series of small rooms. The hall was restored to its proper form between 1961–3 and is now open at times to the public. There is a spendid wooden roof with its smoke outlet below which is the original open hearth.

There is a legend that in 1483 when Edward Duke of Buckingham was executed in Blue Boar Row in Salisbury, his head was taken to King's House. In one room there are stains on the floorboards that can never be removed and said to have come from the blood dripping from the severed head!

171

*OPPOSITE: The north Canonry, view from the garden.*
*ABOVE: The Wardrobe—now the Duke of Edinburgh's Royal Regiment Museum.*

### North Canonry

This was the site of one of the original canonical houses and there are remains of a thirteenth-century crypt, and gables and windows of the fifteenth and seventeenth centuries. It was rebuilt in about 1565 by Canon Robert Hooper whose initials are on shields either side of the entrance arch. The house was rebuilt in the nineteenth century and Hall's 'Picturesque Memorials of Salisbury' of 1835 shows a print of the building, remarking that it 'had, of late years, lost some of its more primitive features'. One feature that still remains to some extent is the garden that runs down to the river. At one time this was renowned as containing one of the finest herbaceous borders in England. It ceased to be a canonical house in 1940. With its projecting bay and fine entrance arch it is a building that thrusts itself into view.

### The Wardrobe

The name derives from the origins of the building in 1254 as the Bishop's Storehouse. The bishop had possession of the building until the sixteenth century when Bishop Jewel exchanged it for the 'glasshouse' which stood on the south side of the cathedral. Little remains of the original house except for foundations and a small section of the basement. Early in the nineteenth century it was extensively altered. In 1835 Hall's 'Picturesque Memorials of Salisbury' remarks: 'Now occupied by Dr. Grove, was repaired, with great judgment and effort, by its late owner, Mr. James Lacy.' It would appear that the work was done to Lacy's design. From 1945–69 it was part of the training college and at the present time is the Museum of the Duke of Edinburgh's Regiment.

## Wren Hall

This was completed in 1714 under the supervision of Thomas Naish, the cathedral clerk of the works, from a design by either Wren or one of his pupils. There is a suggestion that its cost was funded by Stephen Fox who also paid for a church and almshouses at Farley which bear the mark of the same designer.

The Hall is a double classroom with raised masters' desks at either end. There is a dado of wood panelling on which are carved many boys' names. This building and the house joining it to the south formed the choristers' school until 1946, when the school moved to the palace. Dora Robertson's book 'Sarum Close' gives a remarkable insight into school life and conditions from the thirteenth to the twentieth century. The Hall has a sub-basement together with steps leading to a lead canopied entrance. It borders a square of grass known as Choristers' Green, a playground for the boys and at one time home for a cow given by a precentor of the cathedral to ensure a supply of fresh milk for the boys.

## Hemyngsby

In some ways this is like King's House, being a mixture of styles. It can be seen that the left-hand section with its steps leading from a small formal garden is an eighteenth-century southward extension. The right-hand section with its protruding north wing is a mixture of thirteenth- to sixteenth-century work. The first house was built in 1322 by Canon Alexander of Hemingby, who was the first recorded warden of the choristers' school.

The first extension came in the fifteenth century when Nicholas Upton started the work and Canon Fidion (d. 1472) finished it. Fidion has ensured his lasting memory in the

*Hemyngsby in the north-west corner of the Close. The fourteenth-century chapel is seen at the right of the building.*

woodwork of the fifteenth-century hall. His name forms part of the decorative frieze. The northern projection was occupied by a chapel on the first floor connected by a staircase to its entrance on the ground floor. The entrance into the northern part of the house is through a small informal garden and through a small porch against walls containing a mixture of flint brick and stone, a mellow mixture in contrast to the eighteenth-century formality adjoining.

### Mompesson House

This house is now in the care of the National Trust and is open at various times throughout the year. It has a well-propor-

175

tioned stone front with a paved area inside flanking stone piers and a fine set of eighteenth-century iron railings. The house was built about 1680 by Thomas Mompesson and improved by his son, another Thomas, in 1701. Again there is a possible connection with Wren, or one of his pupils; the truth may be that his style was in favour and much copied.

For some time it was used as a lodging for the judges at the assize court. From 1947 to 1951 it was the bishop's residence after the initial move from the palace. In 1952 the house was presented to the National Trust by Denis Martineau.

### Matrons College

This building stands just inside the High Street Gate. A contract dated 8 March 1682 was drawn up with Thomas Glover of Harnham to build the college for the sum of £793.12s.8d. Bishop Seth Ward was the founder of this home for clergy widows from the dioceses of Salisbury and Exeter. The house that previously occupied this site, Clownes Chantry, was bought by the bishop and demolished. The specification for the building work is very detailed: the house to be one hundred and twenty feet (36.6 m) long and to be in the form of an H. There were to be twenty rooms on each floor and eight oak staircases. As Bishop Ward was a friend of Christopher Wren it has been suggested that he was responsible for the design. There is no proof of this, and it was Thomas Naish, the clerk of the works, who supervized the building work.

The College was endowed with land around Salisbury, also in Dorset, Berkshire, Middlesex and the City of London. After its completion, Bishop Ward set out rules governing the conditions and behaviour of the ten matrons. Each was to have her own garden and share the pump and the privy. They were to behave themselves reverently towards their superiors and soberly and respectfully towards each other. The College gates were to be locked at 8 pm each evening and each Saturday the Treasurer was to pay each Widow six shillings pocket money.

Externally the building remains exactly as it was completed in 1683 but internally the accommodation has been improved and altered to accommodate eight matrons instead of ten. Over the doorway is a plaque commemorating Bishop Ward's generous act. In 1980 the building immediately south of the College was divided into seven flats and incorporated into the College to extend the number of places available for 'matrons'.

## No. 21, 'Aula le Stage'

At the halfway point along the north walk stands a house with double gables built of flint with stone dressings. This was a canon's house from 1316 to 1850. At the north-west corner is the 'tower' or upper storey from which the house got its name. In the west end of the house is a fourteenth-century room that was once a chapel. There are also traces of work carried out when Thomas Bennett lived there between 1543–58. Some decorated plaster with rose and pomegranate motifs dates from Bennett's period.

A survey in 1440 revealed the need for repairs and that some of the fixtures were missing, including one great furnace for melting lead!

James Procter occupied the house between 1566 and 1584. He seems to have stripped out panelling, cupboards and furniture, all belonging to the Dean and Chapter, and sold them for his own gain. In the garden is a recess in which there is a memorial to Archdeacon Coxe, who died in 1828. The house was divided into flats in 1980.

## No. 9

This house is on the corner of the north walk and Bishops' Walk. It is a sixteenth-century house on medieval foundations, refronted in the eighteenth century. In the hall is some of the seventeenth-century woodwork from the choir of the cathedral, being part of the prebendal stalls. It is painted white with gold lettering and gives an indication of what the choir furniture looked like at the end of the seventeenth century.

## No. 12

Here on the right-hand side of the road leading to St Ann's Gate lived the Vicars Choral. Their job was to chant and intone the services in the cathedral. They proved at times to be most troublesome and undisciplined, engaging their attention with drink, women and dogs more than their service to the cathedral!

## Malmesbury House

To the north of St Ann's Gate is Malmesbury House, once known as Cole Abbey or Copt Hall. It was built in its present form in the seventeenth and eighteenth century on the site of some small medieval houses. Here lived James Harris, author of 'Hermes' and father of the first Earl of Malmesbury. Inside there are some fine rooms and the house is open to the public at certain times. While at Malmesbury House Harris entertained Handel, who gave concerts in the room over St Ann's Gate. On the south wall of the house is a large sundial inscribed: 'Life is but a walking shadow.' In the garden is a seventeenth-century summerhouse with a 'hiding hole'. The east wall of the house has been incorporated in the Close Wall.

Salisbury is more than just a cathedral: it is a union of Church, Close and City, all of which was planned as one unit.

# BISHOPS OF SALISBURY

| | |
|---|---|
| 1075 | Herman |
| 1078–99 | Osmund |
| 1107–1139 | Roger |
| 1142–1184 | Jocelin de Bohun |
| 1189 | Hubert Walter |
| 1194 | Herbert Poore |
| 1217 | Richard Poore |
| 1229 | Robert Bingham |
| 1247 | William of York |
| 1257 | Giles de Bridport |
| 1263–71 | Walter de la Wyle |
| 1274 | Robert de Wykehampton |
| 1284 | Walter Scammel |
| 1287 | Henry de Braundeston |
| 1289 | William de la Corner |
| 1292 | Nicholas Longespée |
| 1297 | Simon of Ghent |
| 1315 | Roger Mortival |
| 1330 | Robert Wyville |
| 1375 | Ralph Erghum |
| 1388 | John Waltham |
| 1396 | Richard Mitford |
| 1407 | Nicholas Bubwith |
| 1408 | Robert Hallam |
| 1417 | John Chandler |
| 1427 | Robert Neville |
| 1438 | William Aiscough |
| 1450 | Richard Beauchamp |
| 1482 | Lionel Woodville |
| 1485 | Thomas Langton |
| 1494 | John Blyth |
| 1500 | Henry Dean |
| 1502 | Edmund Audley |
| 1525 | Lorenzo Campegio |
| 1535 | Nicholas Shaxton |
| 1539–57 | John Salcot (alias Capon) |
| 1560 | John Jewel |
| 1571 | Edmund Gheast |
| 1577–89 | John Piers |

| | |
|---|---|
| 1591–96 | John Coldwell |
| 1598 | Henry Cotton |
| 1615 | Robert Abbot |
| 1618 | Martin Fotherby |
| 1620 | Robert Townson |
| 1621 | John Davenant |
| 1641 | Brian Duppa |
| 1660 | Humphrey Henchman |
| 1663 | John Earles |
| 1665 | Alexander Hyde |
| 1667 | Seth Ward |
| 1689 | Gilbert Burnet |
| 1715 | William Talbot |
| 1721 | Richard Willis |
| 1723 | Benjamin Hoadly |
| 1734 | Thomas Sherlock |
| 1748 | John Gilbert |
| 1757 | John Thomas |
| 1761 | Robert Hay Drummond |
| 1761 | John Thomas |
| 1766 | John Hume |
| 1782 | Shute Barrington |
| 1791 | John Douglas |
| 1807 | John Fisher |
| 1825 | Thomas Burgess |
| 1837 | Edward Denison |
| 1854 | Walter Kerr Hamilton |
| 1869 | George Moberly |
| 1885 | John Wordsworth |
| 1911 | Frederick Ridgeway |
| 1921 | St Clair Donaldson |
| 1936 | Neville Lovett |
| 1946 | Geoffrey Lunt |
| 1949 | William Anderson |
| 1963 | Joseph Fison |
| 1973 | George Reindorp |
| 1982 | John Austin Baker |

# DEANS OF SALISBURY

| | |
|---|---|
| c. 1091 | Walter |
| c. 1098 | Roger |
| c. 1102 | Osbert |
| c. 1108 | Serlo |
| c. 1109 | Robert |
| 1112 | Robert Chichester |
| 1140 | Robert Warlewast |
| 1155 | Henry de Beaumont (de Bellomonte) |
| c. 1165 | Azo (or Atso) |
| 1166 | John of Oxford (de Oxeneford) |
| 1176 | Jordan |
| 1195 | Eustace |
| 1198 | Richard Poore |
| 1215 | Adam of Ilchester |
| 1220 | William de Wenda (or Wanda) |
| 1237 | Robert de Hertford |
| 1258 | Robert de Wykehampton |
| 1274 | Walter Scammel |
| 1284 | Henry de Braundeston |
| 1288 | Symon de Micham (or Michelham) |
| 1297 | Peter de Savoy (de Sabaudia) |
| 1309 | William Cardinal Priest of S. Pudentiana |
| 1311 | Reymund de la Goth (or 'de Fargis') |
| 1347 | Bertrand de la Goth (or 'de Fargis') |
| c. 1347 | Reginald 'Ursinus' (or 'de Filiis Ursi') |
| c. 1376 | James Ursinus |
| 1379 | Robert Braybrook |
| 1382 | Thomas Montacute |
| 1404 | John Chandler |
| 1418 | Simon Sydenham |
| 1431 | Thomas Browne |
| 1435 | Nicholas Billesden |
| 1441 | Adam Moleyns |
| 1446 | Richard Leyott |
| 1449 | Gilbert Kymer |
| 1463 | James Goldwell |
| 1473 | John Davyson |
| 1486 | Edward Cheyne |
| 1502 | Thomas Rowthall |

| 1509 | William Atwater |
|------|-----------------|
| 1514 | John Longlands |
| 1521 | Cuthbert Tunstall |
| 1523 | Reymund Pade |
| 1540 | Peter Vannes |
| 1563 | William Bradbridge |
| 1570 | Edmund Freake |
| 1571 | John Piers |
| 1578 | John Bridges |
| 1605 | John Gordon |
| 1619 | John Williams |
| 1620 | John Bowle |
| 1630 | Edmund Mason |
| 1635 | Richard Baylie |
| 1667 | Ralph Brideoake |
| 1675 | Thomas Pierce |
| 1691 | Robert Woodward |
| 1702 | Edward Young |
| 1705 | John Younger |
| 1728 | John Clarke |
| 1757 | Thomas Greene |
| 1780 | Rowney Noel |
| 1786 | John Eykins |
| 1809 | Charles Talbot |
| 1823 | Hugh Nicolas Pearson |
| 1846 | Francis Lear |
| 1850 | Henry Parr Hamilton |
| 1880 | George David Boyle |
| 1901 | Allan Becher Webb |
| 1907 | William Page Roberts |
| 1920 | Andrew Ewbank Burn |
| 1928 | John Hugh Granville Randolph |
| 1936 | Edward Lowry Henderson |
| 1943 | Henry Charles Robins |
| 1952 | Robert Hamilton Moberly |
| 1960 | Kenneth William Haworth |
| 1971 | William Fenton Morley |
| 1977 | Sydney Hall Evans |
| 1986 | Hugh Geoffrey Dickinson |

# ACKNOWLEDGEMENTS AND BIBLIOGRAPHY

Having been connected with Salisbury Cathedral for some eighteen years, it has become part of my life. Despite my attachment to the cathedral, only when showing others around it, or writing about it, do I once again recapture the first impressions that Salisbury made on me. For this reason I am grateful to Unwin Hyman for giving me the opportunity to write this book

My thanks must go also to my wife, Jean, who has kept me in line with encouragement and general assistance, Hilary Jobling for unflagging typing, Suzanne Eward, the Librarian and Keeper of the Muniments, for information about the library, to the Dean and Chapter and to the many members of the cathedral's community for their interest in the project.

The list of books consulted, which the reader may also like to consult for an extension of the information contained within this book, are:

**A Description of Salisbury Cathedral** by Francis Price
Published 1747, reprinted in enlarged form 1774.

**Salisbury Cathedral** by William Dodsworth
Published 1814

**Salisbury Cathedral** by John Britton
Published 1814

**Picturesque Memorials of Salisbury** by Rev. Peter Hall
Published 1834

**Fasti Ecclesiae Sarisberiensis** by William Jones
Published 1879

**Altering Ancient Cathedrals** by Rev. John Milner
Published 1811

**Sarum Close** by Dora H. Robertson
Published by Jonathan Cape 1938

**Salisbury Cathedral** by Kathleen Edwards
an Ecclesiastical History, reprinted
from the Victoria County History of Wiltshire, Volume III,
published by O.U.P.

**The Stained Glass of Salisbury Cathedral** by R. O. C. Spring
Published by the Friends of Salisbury Cathedral

**Salisbury City, Volume 1**
by Royal Commission on Historical Monuments
Published 1980 by H.M.S.O.

Various pamphlets produced by the Friends of the Cathedral
and articles from their annual publication 'The Spire'.
Guide books published by Brown and Co. of Salisbury
at various dates during the second half of the nineteenth century

The photographs in this book are mainly the work of myself and Joe Proctor with the exception of the following:
British Crown Copyright/A&AEE Photographs 9, 37, 39, 51, 54; George Hall 33, 69, 97, 100, 140, 147, 153; John McCann 59; Royal Commission on the Historical Monuments of England 7, 31, 50, 73, 94, 115, 117, 134.

# Glossary

AISLE A longitudinal division of nave or choir. In the large churches used as a processional path.

AMBULATORY Walkway for processions. Usually used to describe the processional path behind the high altar dividing it from the eastern chapels.

APSE Semi-circular termination to the eastern end of chapel or church.

ARCADE A series of arches supported by columns or piers, either open or backed by masonry.

ARCH A construction of brick or stone over an opening, so arranged as to be self-supporting and able to carry a superimposed weight.

ASHLAR Squared stones used in building work.

AUMBRY A cupboard, usually near an altar, in which the Sacrament is kept.

BALL-FLOWER A carved ornament resembling a ball placed in a three-petalled circular flower.

BAND A continuous 'series' of ornaments in a wall. An intermediate moulding encircling a pillar or shaft.

BAPTISTRY A separate building or part of a building where baptisms and Christenings take place.

BASE The lower part of a pier or shaft, the usually moulded stone upon which the pier or shafts sits. The lower part of a wall where there is a moulded enlargement.

BATTLEMENT An indented parapet, the rising parts termed merlons and the opening crenels or embrasures.

BAY A principal compartment or division in the architectural arrangement of a building.

BED A mason's term to describe the direction in which the natural strata in stones lies. Also the term for the top and bottom surfaces of a stone.

BENCH-TABLE A low stone seat on the inside of walls.

BOSS The carved key-stone in vaulting work.

BRASSES Monumental plates of brass or latten inlaid into stone slabs and engraved with pictures and words commemorating a deceased person.

BUTTRESS A projection from a wall to create additional strength and support. Those rising beyond the top of a wall with an arched projection to support a wall at a higher level are flying buttresses.

CAMPANILE A name adopted from the Italian for a bell-tower. Can be either attached to a building or a separate building as at Chichester and Chester.

CANOPY A projecting cover over an altar, statue, choir-stalls or any other object.

CAPITAL The head of a pier, column, shaft etc.

CATHEDRAL The principal church of a diocese in which the Bishop's cathedra or throne is placed.

CHANCEL The choir or eastern part of a church.

CHANTRY An ecclesiastical benefice or endowment to provide for the offering of masses for the soul of the person who endowed the chantry. In most cases a chapel was built in which the person who had provided the endowment was buried.

CHAPTER The governing body of a CATHEDRAL.

CHAPTER HOUSE A meeting room in which the business of a CATHEDRAL was carried out. In some CATHEDRALS this is still so.

CHOIR Not only the singers but the area fitted out for singing. Eastward from the singing area to the high altar is the presbytery.

CLERESTORY Window, row of windows or openings in the upper part of a building.

CLOISTER A covered walkway usually arranged around three or four sides of an open area. The area enclosed by the cloister is the garth.

CLUSTERED COLUMN A pier consisting of many shafts, sometimes attached to each other.

COLUMN A round pillar, the term including the base, shaft and capital.

COPING A course of flat or sloping stones covering the top of a wall.

CORBEL A projecting stone supporting a superimposed weight. The stone is usually moulded and carved.

CROCKETS Projecting leaves, flowers or bunches of foliage used to decorate the angles of spires, canopies, pinnacles etc.

CUSP A point formed by two parts of a curve meeting as in window tracery.

DEAN The appointed head of a CATHEDRAL. Acts as chairman at the meetings of the CATHEDRAL CHAPTER. In the parish-church CATHEDRALS the appointed head is a provost.

DECORATED STYLE The full development of GOTHIC ARCHITECTURE spanning the period between EARLY ENGLISH and PERPENDICULAR.

EARLY ENGLISH STYLE The first of the pointed or GOTHIC styles of architecture used in this country. It succeeded the Norman at the end of the twelfth century and merged with the DECORATED at the end of the thirteenth.

ESCUTCHEON A shield charged with armorial bearings.

FACADE A term adopted from the French for the exterior face or front of a building.

FAN-TRACERY VAULTING A kind of vaulting developed in late PERPENDICULAR work, in which all the ribs that rise from the springing of the vault have the same curve and diverge equally in every direction producing an effect like an open fan.

FINIAL A carved termination to pinnacles, canopies etc.

FOIL-ARCH An arch formed of a series of small arches. A prefix designates the number of arches used, i.e. trefoil, cinquefoil etc.

FRONTAL A hanging with which the front of an altar is covered.

GARGOYLE A projecting spout, usually carved, used to throw water clear of a building.

GOTHIC ARCHITECTURE The term GOTHIC is of modern usage but it covers the style of design in building work that developed from the late 12thC to the early 16th. Divided roughly into three: EARLY ENGLISH, DECORATED and PERPENDICULAR.

HIGH ALTAR The principal altar in a church.

HOLY WATER STOUP A receptacle for holy water placed near the entrance of churches.

HOOD MOULDING Projecting moulding over the heads of arches, also known as the dripstone.

JAMB The side of a window, door or chimney.

JESSE Tree of Jesse – a representation of the genealogy of Christ, in which the different persons forming the descent are placed in foliage scrolls to form a tree. Representations found in windows, carved stone, manuscripts etc.

LADY CHAPEL A chapel dedicated to the Blessed Virgin Mary. Usually situated at the eastern end of a church. There are exceptions as at Ely where the Lady Chapel projects from the north transept.

LANTERN A term usually applied to

part or all of the interior of a tower open to the church below.

LAVATORY A cistern or trough to wash in.

LEDGER A large flat stone as placed over a tomb or burial place.

LIERNE A rib of a vault that crosses between other ribs and does not rise from the springing point or contacts the ridge rib.

LIGHTS The openings between the mullions of a window.

LINTEL A piece of timber or stone placed horizontally over a window or door opening.

LOZENGE A diamond shape formed by mouldings or as in leaded glazing.

MERLON The solid part of an embattled PARAPET.

MISERERE The projecting bracket on the underside of the seats of stalls in churches. The projection formed a ledge which gave relief during long periods of standing. Most have some form of carving upon them.

MOSAIC WORK Ornamental work formed by inlaying pieces, usually cubes, of glass and stone.

MOULDING A general term to cover any assemblage of narrow surfaces projecting from a wall.

MULLION The slender pier that forms the vertical divisions in a window.

NAVE The main western section of a church.

NICHE A recess in a wall for a statue or other ornament.

PARAPET A low wall used to protect the gutters or roof of a building.

PARVIS A name now given to a small room over a porch. Some such rooms were used as libraries in parish churches.

PERPENDICULAR STYLE The last of the styles of GOTHIC architecture covering the period from the last half of the 14thC until the first half of the 16thC.

PIER An isolated mass of masonry, a Saxon term displaced by the French pillar.

PILLAR Usually the masonry that supports an arch in an arcade.

PINNACLE A small spire-like structure, usually four-sided and ornamented, that is placed on the top of buttresses or at the corners of towers.

PISCINA A water-drain, placed near an altar, usually within the thickness of the wall.

PRESBYTERY The part of a church in which the high altar is placed. Usually raised above the level of the rest of the floor.

PULPIT An elevated desk from which sermons are delivered. Not only found in churches but also in the refectories of monasteries, as at Chester and Beaulieu.

PURBECK MARBLE Not a true marble but a shelly limestone from the Isle of Purbeck consisting of the shells of one type of freshwater snail held together with a limestone matrix. Takes a high polish.

PILASTER A square column generally attached to a wall.

PUTLOG A horizontal member in scaffolding sometimes with one end fixed into the wall against which the scaffold is fixed.

PUTLOG HOLE Holes left in masonry walls to receive the ends of putlogs.

QUOIN The external angle of a building.

QUATREFOIL Panels or openings of various shapes divided by cusping into four leaves or sections.

RELIQUARY A small chest, box or casket in which relics of saints were kept.

REREDOS Wall or screen at the rear of an altar.

RIB Moulded stone or wood projecting band on a ceiling or vault.

ROOD BEAM A beam upon which the crucifix is supported.

SACRISTY A room in a church in which the vessels, vestments and other valuables connected with the religious services of the building are, or were, preserved.

SADDLE BARS Metal bars to which leaded glazing is fixed.

SANCTUARY The presbytery or eastern part of the choir of a church.

SEDILIA Latin name for a seat, usually applied to distinguish the seats to the south side of the choir near the altar. Sometimes moveable but usually set within the wall within canopied niches.

SHAFT The body of a column or pier, the section between base and capital.

SPANDREL The triangular space formed where two arches meet or an arch meets a wall.

STALL A fixed seat partially or wholly enclosed.

STOUP Container for holy water placed at the entrance of a church.

SPRINGING The point at which an arch starts its course. The point at which it sits upon a pier or wall.

STRING-COURSE A projecting band or line of mouldings.

TRACERY The pierced work at the head of a window or opening.

TRANSEPT Any part of a church that projects at right angles from it and is of equal, or nearly equal, height to the main building.

TRIFORIUM A gallery or arcade in the wall over pier arches of the main arcade.

TYMPANUM The space between a door lintel and the surrounding arch.

TREFOIL Panel or opening divided by cusps into three sections or leaves.

VAULT A stone or wood ceiling supported by a series of arches or as in a barrel vault the ceiling is one continuous arch.

VESICA A pointed oval shape. Such a shape in stone or glass containing a figure of Christ, the Trinity or the Blessed Virgin Mary.

VESTRY See SACRISTY.

VISE Spiral staircase.

VOUSSOIR The wedge shaped stones of which an arch is constructed.

WALL BENCHING See BENCH-TABLE.

*Thirteenth-century armrest from the choir stalls.*

# INDEX

Bold numerals refer to captions

Aiscough, William, Bishop of
Salisbury 18, 158, **159**
Albany, Duke of: memorial
window 109
Alexander, Canon, of
Hemingby 174
Aprice, John: arms 106
Armfield, Rev H T: *Guide to
the Statues on the West
Front* 32, 40
Assumption of the Blessed
Virgin chapel 19
Aubrey, John 19
on Bishop Ward 137
Audley, Edmund, Bishop of
Salisbury 18, **125**
tomb 123

Bacon, John 121
Baker, Prof Robert 76
Barrington, Shute, Bishop of
Salisbury 168
Beauchamp chantry chapel 10,
18, 44, **45**, 80, 86, 87, 119,
146, 165
demolished, eighteenth c 22
Beauchamp, Earl 102
Beauchamp, Richard, Bishop
of Salisbury 10, 18, 70, 87,
168
remains 112
Beare, John 106
Bell, James 109
Bell tower (detached) 162,
**163**
bells 162, 164
fought over in Civil War
162–3
sold and demolished,
eighteenth c 164
use as ale house 163–4
Bennett, Thomas 123, 177
tomb 123
Bertie, W V: memorial 138
Bingham, Robert, Bishop of
Salisbury 13, 138, 165
tomb 125
Bishop's palace 18, 19, 165,
166, 167–8
now Cathedral School 167,
**167**
Blomfield, Arthur 99, **101**, 131
Blyth, John, Bishop of
Salisbury 122
tomb 43, 87, 122
Bouverie, Hon the Rev P B
131
Brewer, Alice 14
Bridport, Giles de, Bishop of
Salisbury 13, 34, 133
tomb 88, 133, **134**, 135
Britton, John 129
memorial 121
on Salisbury's spire 121
Bryant, Sir Arthur 170
floor slab 67
Burgess, Thomas, Bishop of
Salisbury: tomb 137
Burne-Jones, Edward 109

Byng, Hon John 164
on Salisbury Cathedral,
1782 21

Calixtus III, Pope 18
Cathedrals' Advisory
Commission 29
Central crossing 68–72
bending of piers 68
Green Man head 70
pulpit 70
shields 70
vault **69**, 70
Chapter House 15, 19, 26, 29,
**46**, 47, 80, 83, 106, 146,
149–50, 152, 154–7
Old Testament frieze 14, 19,
150, 152, **153**, 154–5
'Purity scourging Lust' **148**
stained glass 155, 156
statue at entrance **147**
tiles 155
Tower of Bable carving 152
vaulting 149, **150**
vices and virtues figures 149
Chantrey, Sir Francis 122
Charles I 121
Charles II 58
Cheney, Sir John 87, 118, 138
tomb 118–19
Chicheley, Henry, Archbishop
of Canterbury 168
Choir 21, 95–6, 98–103
carved angels on choir stalls
**100**
commemorative plaques 102
organ case 100
painted vault 96, **96**
piers 95
present altar 102–3
pulpit 102
screen 70–1, 90
stained glass 110
stall canopies 99–100, 101
**101**
subjects of paintings 98
thirteenth c carved armrest
**99**
thirteenth c winch 98
woodwork 98–100, 102
Cloisters 47, 139, 141, **141**,
143, 145–6
buttresses 141 **142**
cedars of Lebanon **145**, 146
entrances 143, 146
panel depicting St Michael
141, 143, **144**
plumbery 143
screen 141
Close 161–7
'Aula le Stage' (no 21) 177
Choristers Green 174
churchyard 21, 164–5, 167
Constable 167
gates 165–6
Hemingsby (house) 174–5
**175**
King's House—Old Deanery
**170**, 170–1

Leadenhall—'Aula Plumbea'
168–9, **169**
Malmesbury House 166,
177
Matron's College 122, 176
Mompesson House 175–6
Myles Place (No 68) 170
No 9 177
No 12 177–8
North Canonry **173**, 173
Walks 167, 177
wall 165
Walton Canonry (No 69)
169–70
Wardrobe **173**, 173–4
Whitsun Fair 58, 164
Wren Hall 174
Clutton, Henry 26, 156
College of de Vaux 133, 165
Constable, John 168
Corfe, Thomas: memorial 146
Coxe, Archdeacon 177
Cyrcetur, Thomas 159

De Burgh, Hubert 116
Defoe, Daniel
*Journey through England*
96
on Salisbury Cathedral 96,
100–1
Denison, Edward, Bishop of
Salisbury 26
Dodsworth, William 64, 119,
145–6
grave 145
on Hertford tomb 129
on Lord Hungerford's
remains 112, 114
on Wyatt's use of limewash
77, 79
Duke of Edinburgh's Royal
Regiment Museum **173**,
174

Earle, William Benson:
monument 122
Eastern end **11**, **25**, **39**, 43–4
Edward IV 122
Edward VI 129, 136
Elias of Dereham 12–13, 157,
168, **169**
Elizabeth I 127, 129, 130
Elizabeth II 102, 166
Erghum, Ralph, Bishop of
Salisbury 17, 66
Evans, Dean Sydney Hall 109
Eyre, Francis 169

Fidion, Canon 174–5
Fiennes, Celia: on Salisbury
Cathedral, 1682 95–6
Fisher, Archdeacon John 168
Fisher, John, Bishop of
Salisbury: monument 138
Flaxman, John 122
Fletcher, Canon 129, 135
Fletcher, Mrs Morris 90
Folkerzheimer, Herman: on
Bishop's palace, 1563 168

189